Praise for Gospel Patrons

I read this book from cover to cover in two days. I couldn't put it down. The three stories of generous givers and their impact on the spread of the gospel in history are compelling. I am praying for thousands of similar "Gospel Patrons" for our generation!

Todd Harper
President of Generous Giving

This is a great read! I love the way these stories paint a picture of stewarding relationship, affluence and influence to lay up treasure in heaven. Sharing powerful stories like those found in Gospel Patrons is the most effective way to encourage the kind of kingdom engagement we are so excited to see today.

David Wills
President of the National Christian Foundation

John Rinehart has given us a wonderfully stirring portrait of gospel partnerships used mightily by God at key turning points in evangelical history. This is a great model for Gospel Patronage today, for we urgently need new generations of courageous preachers. And they in turn need the sacrificial sponsorship and friendship of patrons who share the same burden for lost souls and love for the Saviour.

Colin Marshall
Author of The Trellis and the Vine and CEO of Vinegrowers

What a beautiful and timely form of encouragement for those of us so inclined to press deeper into strategic, long-term relationships around our gifting and the gifting of others to bring about flourishing. Such a rich heritage and legacy that has been time-tested to bear much fruit. Count Marla and me in for this generation, we are moved to be Gospel Patrons!

Tim & Marla Krupa
Entrepreneur and Chairman of the Board, Center for
Missional Entrepreneurship

This is a stirring account of some of the great unsung heroes of the faith, whose hidden sacrificial giving has been so crucial in the work of evangelism. I pray the Lord will use it to inspire a new generation of Gospel Patrons.

Vaughan Roberts
Rector of St Ebbe's, Oxford, UK and Director of the Proclamation Trust

Gospel Patrons are about changing people's eternal destiny. If we are to take the gospel to a dying world, we desperately need a new generation of deliberate, generous, and joyful men and women who will be patrons and partners in gospel preaching. This book not only gives examples of how God has used Gospel Patrons in past centuries, but it also challenges a new generation to step up into being patrons.

Al Stewart
Director of the Geneva Push church-planting network and Chairman of Katoomba Christian Convention, Sydney, Australia

Over the centuries the Lord has wonderfully raised up Christians with the means and the zeal to give very generously. While others do conventional things with their money, these people do remarkable things in oiling the wheels that carry God's Word and end up having an influence more supernatural than natural.

You could read this heart-warming book by John Rinehart and love the gospel. You could read it and long to spread the gospel. But if you read it and join that great line of "Gospel Patrons" — some are described in this book — the world will (seriously) not be the same again.

Simon Manchester
Senior Minister, St Thomas' Anglican Church, North Sydney, Australia

Here is a unique and thought-provoking book. With biblical exhortation and powerful examples from church history, John Rinehart presents us with a vision of the enormous potential for gospel usefulness by means of generous and focused financial and practical support for front-line Christian workers. We find here a responsibility that few of us dare ignore. Let us then take up the challenge that confronts us in these pages and experience a great joy in seeing Christ's cause advance both in our own countries and in some of the far-flung places of the earth.

Faith Cook
Author of Selina Countess of Huntingdon

This splendid book provides great encouragement to Christians to maximise their resources for gospel ministry. It is not only challenging, but also inspiring. May God use it to raise up a generation of Gospel Patrons.

William Taylor
Rector of St Helen's Church Bishopsgate, London, UK

John Rinehart draws our attention to the vital role played by the often comparatively unknown sponsors of well-known gospel servants. Through their quiet generosity, these Gospel Patrons helped to change the world. Rinehart's message is plain — that we could and should imitate their example today. As John Newton wrote: "Surely there is nothing worth living for but to be instrumental in promoting His service."

Marylynn Rouse
Director of The John Newton Project

God places His redemptive purposes in the dreams and visions of available servants whose commitment to His glory is often unto death. When I ponder how He must love them and ultimately welcome them into His presence, I aspire to be within their band of brothers and sisters. What an immense, fulfilling privilege it is to find those partners whose good works I have been ordained to serve. In this inspiring compilation, John Rinehart provides compelling proof that all things are possible with God when His presence, power and provision become a three stranded cord.

Jay Bennett
Vice Chair of the National Christian Foundation

Gospel Patrons

Gospel
Patrons

People Whose Generosity
Changed the World

John Rinehart

RECLAIMED
PUBLISHING

FIRST EDITION

Published by Reclaimed Publishing. Reclaimed Publishing is a division of Reclaimed, Inc. For more information or to contact Reclaimed Publishing visit: http://www.reclaimedpublishing.com

Cover Design & Artwork by John-Mark Warkentin, http://www.jmwarkentin.com

Printed and bound by The Avery Group at Shapco Printing, Inc., Minneapolis

ISBN: 978-1-4675-9398-4

For Jesus,
who wrote my name in His book!

Contents

Foreword

By Bob Shank
Founder of The Master's Program

I have spent twenty five years trying to help people discover their "Kingdom Calling." Many of them have been marketplace leaders and business and professional men and women. And what I've seen in the overlap of business and ministry is that both are team sports.

In the latter part of the twentieth century, a name was given to a category of investor that had long played a role in business, but had lacked a suitable moniker. The title "Angel Investor" was coined to describe an often-invisible contributor to entrepreneurial success. Angel Investors are a hybrid blend of financier and mentor. The financier dimension points toward the business plan and the product or service that defines the enterprise; the mentor relationship points toward the fledgling founder who has a dream, but lacks the discernment honed through years of real-life experience in the trenches. The Angel Investor provides enterprise funding and entrepreneurial finishing that helps the start-up reach levels of sustainability and scalability that would have been unlikely otherwise.

The role of an Angel Investor is seldom spotlighted and not easily explained to a broad audience, but for the early-stage business creator, these investors are forever celebrated as a senior partner in the company's ultimate success. The marketplace hero seldom reaches the pinnacle alone; it takes a team to reach the summit.

Ministry is the same. God loves to do great things, but most of His work He does through people, and it is His design for people to thrive when matched with other people who bring their unique capability to the effort. In a culture of individuality that's obsessed with heroes, it's easy to forget that God works through the Body of Christ: the collection of collaborators who each offer their unique gifts, talents and distinctions to the effort that results in the glory of God and the expansion of His kingdom. Ministry—by God's design—is a team sport.

You could revisit the missionary journeys of the apostle Paul and imagine him working alone, but the contemporaries who experienced his ministry to the Gentiles saw him alongside his early-stage partner, Barnabas. In fact, when the polytheists in the city of Lystra saw the power of God manifested in their midst, they mistook Barnabas as Zeus— the "father of gods and men" to the Greco/Roman religious observer—and they presumed Paul to be Hermes—the son of Zeus, and the spokesman for that more powerful deity. Clearly, Barnabas was no incidental part of the missional partnership who had arrived with the gospel (Acts 14:8–14).

Barnabas' role in the early church made him aware of the unusual financial challenges in supporting the Pentecost pilgrims who had come to the city for their festival and had found faith in the Messiah. They stayed with their travel possessions that were exhausted and then became dependent on the hospitality of the local believers. Barnabas was not simply an observer or verbalizer. He acted to meet the extraordinary need with extraordinary generosity. He sold a piece of property that he owned and transferred the funds to the apostles for immediate assistance in caring for the new Christians.

Paul is the celebrated champion of the first-century faith, but his story would have unfolded far differently without the significant involvement of Barnabas alongside him. Barnabas may be one of the earliest examples of a Gospel Patron. The investment his time, his gifts and talents, his relationships and reputation, and his involvement in Paul's unfolding ministry life and leadership is a powerful picture of a Gospel Patron's engagement in the big picture of God's plan.

But let's not simply look back in history to marvel at the unsung heroes who played an integral part in some of the massive milestones of God's kingdom on earth. Instead, let's look to the future and ask ourselves how God might have us place our discretionary time, talents, growing influence and generous giving alongside a Gideon, a David, a Daniel, a Paul, a Tyndale, a Whitefield, or a Newton? How might our mentoring and our investing join forces to cause a beneficent breakthrough that would not happen without a Gospel Patron? As the stories in this short but powerful account will show, Gospel Patrons demonstrate a commitment to another leader that links them at the calling level.

There are many people who pray that God will raise up leaders for His Kingdom in our generation who could be used by Him to accelerate the completion of the Great Commission. After considering the stories in this book, you may feel called to pray that God will raise up Gospel Patrons—to align with the more obvious and outspoken leaders—who will add the catalytic spark that brings astounding works of God into the flow of human history.

I hope you enjoy this retelling of the people whose bold bets on God's champions gave us the Christian faith we share today!

And through his faith,
though he died, he still speaks.

HEBREWS 11:4

1 The Discovery

John
Rinehart

Sometimes we need to read history so that we don't repeat it. Other times we need to read it so that we do.

I'm writing this book because I believe our generation's greatest need is for history to be repeated. Five hundred years ago a mighty reformation shook Europe, and subsequently, the world. Two hundred and fifty years ago a powerful evangelical revival awakened millions in the colonies that would become the United States of America. Today, in the twenty-first century, I pray God will again touch down and give the masses a fresh sense that He's real and true.

I dream of seeing churches overflow with crowds of people who are hungry to learn the Bible. I envision businessmen strategizing together about how to advance the gospel because their greatest passion is Jesus. I imagine college students gathering to talk about our great salvation and how they can spend their lives extending it to others.

I picture Christians being marked by radical generosity and risk-taking action to see more lives changed, more souls saved, and more people sent around the world to reach the unreached. I envision more preachers proclaiming the great doctrines of the Bible with unstoppable courage, while God draws many to the Savior. I dream of thousands of people discovering their calling in God's eternal kingdom and then running hard to play their part well.

How would our world be different if we lived like the real business of life was to love God and help as many people as possible learn to love Him too? What if we recaptured a sense of urgency to live for eternity?

I desire this. I long to see God revive our generation.

The conviction driving this book is that God works through people to change the world—and He's not done yet. I believe our world can be different, and I believe God wants to work through us to make it different.

The aim of this book is to ask and answer two very important questions: First, *How has God worked through people to change the world?* And second, *How do we become those kind of people?*

I began to find my way toward answering these questions on a sunny November morning in Sydney, Australia.

The Story of Gospel Patronage

My wife and I stepped into an elevator filled with people dressed in blue and black suits, pushed the circular button for floor 31, and waited. When the doors opened we approached the receptionist and stated our names. A few minutes later a silver-haired businessman named Simon emerged through the double doors.

"John and Renée, lovely to meet you," he said. "Shall we head downstairs for a cup of coffee?"

Our meeting with Simon had been arranged by a mutual friend who thought I might be interested to learn about something called Gospel Patronage. I had no idea what that term meant, so as we chatted, I asked him directly, "Simon, I was told I should ask you about Gospel Patronage. What is it?"

"My own story," Simon said, "began several years ago as I was about to launch a new company. I realized that if the business succeeded then I stood to make a lot of money. I also knew I needed a strategy in place to be able to prosper financially without failing spiritually. So I began to look for examples in history and soon found that when God raised up preachers and missionaries to lead the great movements of the gospel, He also raised up patrons to come alongside those leaders as partners in the work.

"For example," Simon continued, "in the 1500s an Englishman named William Tyndale wanted to translate the Bible from the original Greek and Hebrew into English. For 1,000 years the Bible had been locked in Latin, but most Englishmen couldn't read Latin and therefore did not know the Bible. Tyndale wanted to change that. He wanted his countrymen to meet the God of the Bible, a God they had heard about but never known. The problem was Bible translation was illegal; you could be killed for it. But God intervened through a godly businessman named Humphrey Monmouth. Monmouth protected Tyndale, he provided for him, and he even used his merchant ships to smuggle the first English New Testaments throughout England. Very few people have ever heard of Monmouth, but his partnership with Tyndale changed the world."

I was spellbound and couldn't wait to learn more about these backstage VIPs, who Simon called "Gospel Patrons." Humphrey

Monmouth called Tyndale off the bench and put him in the game. What drove people like that? What made them so different from the average church-goers of their day and ours? They weren't content to be spectators; instead, they engaged. Simon's stories painted a picture I had never seen, and I was eager to share it with others.

An Electric Response

After a week's vacation in Sydney, we left to be home for Christmas in Seattle. Once among family and friends, I repeated everything I could remember about Monmouth and another patron named John Thornton. The responses shocked me.

"Can you tell my wife those stories," a friend asked, "and a few of my business partners too?"

"What was the name of that thing you talked about?" my sister questioned, "I want to tell my friends about it."

My father-in-law listened intently and returned to the subject days later. Gospel Patronage was electric.

I began to dig a little deeper and soon found that Gospel Patronage has a look-a-like that has also been electric. The special thirtieth anniversary issue of *Forbes* magazine trumpeted "The Titans of Philanthropy." Philanthropy has found its way onto many magazine covers and television screens in recent years—and for good reason.

In 2000, the Bill & Melinda Gates Foundation was launched with an asset base of $16 billion. In 2005, former U.S. President Bill Clinton established the Clinton Global Initiative, which has received billions of dollars in commitments from government leaders, leading CEOs, and major philanthropists. In 2006, the second-richest man in the United States, Warren Buffett, announced his plan to give away the vast majority of his fortune of more than $40 billion to philanthropic causes. Lately, Gates and Buffett have teamed up to challenge the wealthiest 400 Americans, all billionaires, "to pledge...at least 50% of their net worth to charity during their lifetimes or at death."[1] Executives, celebrities, and politicians all want to change the world, and some are willing to pay for it.

On the surface, philanthropists sound a lot like Gospel Patrons. Both emphasize giving. Both want to make a difference in the world. Both would acknowledge that a great life is not built on what you gain, but on what you give your life to accomplish.[2] But philanthropists and Gospel Patrons aim at very different targets.

The titans of philanthropy will be remembered for giving to good causes; Gospel Patrons will be remembered for giving to eternal ones. Where philanthropists aim to nourish people's bodies and train their minds, Gospel Patrons prioritize people's souls. Gospel Patrons treat symptoms, but ultimately they go after the disease.

And to cure any disease you must begin with a correct diagnosis. God's diagnosis is that humanity's fundamental problem is not poverty or lack of education. It's not drugs or disease. It's

---

1   Carol J. Loomis, "The $600 Billion Challenge" CNN.com (June 16, 2010), http://features.blogs.fortune.cnn.com/2010/06/16/gates-buffett-600-billion-dollar-philanthropy-challenge/.

2   Bob Shank, *Life Mastery: Discover the Timeless Secrets to Living Life as Jesus Did* (Ventura, Calif.: Regal, 2012), 37.

not capitalism or communism, politics or religion. Our core problem, the Bible says, is that we're all sinners, guilty before God and headed for God's righteous judgment. Like our first parents, Adam and Eve, we turn to our own ways, focus on ourselves, and ignore, neglect, and reject the God who made us. Our relationship with God is broken because of our sin, and the punishment awaiting us is death and hell. That's the bad news—the true diagnosis.

The good news is that God knows we can't save ourselves, and He doesn't ask us to. Even though we act like His enemies, God loves us so much that He sent His son Jesus to die on the cross for us. Jesus exchanged His life for yours and mine. He died in our place for our sins, taking our punishment on Himself, and rescuing us from the judgment we deserve. He is our substitute, our sacrifice, and our savior. And everyone who turns away from their sins and trusts in Jesus will be saved. You don't have to fix yourself or try harder or do better; you simply have to humble yourself, believe that Jesus paid it all and receive His forgiveness and eternal life. This is the cure.

Understanding our true diagnosis and its one remedy leads us to the most loving and lasting cause we can give our lives to. Whether we run a company, lead a department, or answer the phone, our mission is the same: to advance the message that Jesus saves people who are lost in sin. God is not looking for philanthropists who can write big checks, but for people who love Him and live to spread the news of His son, Jesus.

The Danger of Success

Simon's caution about success was right on target. The pattern we see in the Bible is that success in life often leads to spiritual failure. For example, Noah successfully believed God, built the ark and survived the storm, but then when life was comfortable he drank too much wine and became drunk. Abraham heard God's call to leave his homeland, and he successfully obeyed in faith, but afterward got scared and lied about Sarah, saying she was his sister.

By faith Gideon won an impossible battle with only 300 men, but after his success he made a golden ephod that he, his family, and his country worshiped instead of God. David was a man after God's own heart, and the Lord gave him victory wherever he went. But comfortable in his success David stayed home when he ought to have gone out to battle with his men, and he ended up committing adultery with Bathsheba and ordering the murder of her husband.

We experience success, become comfortable, then forgetful of God, and finally disobedient to Him.[3] Like the Israelites, we eat and are full; we build good houses and live in them; our possessions multiply and our wealth increases, and then we "forget the LORD our God."[4] Success inflates our pride and quietly derails our focus on God.

Thankfully, there is another way, an approach which puts both God and success in their rightful places. The Bible and history show us that our prosperity is not a curse, but an

---

3   See also Ezekiel 28.
4   Deuteronomy 8:11–14.

opportunity—an opportunity I believe many people miss out on.

This book looks to the Bible and church history to reclaim beautiful examples of people who learned to worship and serve God while experiencing prosperity and success. We need the stories of men and women who walked the balance beam of blessing without falling off into self-indulgence or self-righteousness. We need to see how they found the narrow way that leads to life, so we can find it too.

The Real Stories of Real People

I can imagine some of you asking, "But why history? History can be so dry—dates and facts, wars and maps, stuff we don't care about and can't remember anyway."

My eighth-grade history teacher Mr. Martin knew many of us thought this way about history, so he spiced up his lectures with mythical tales about his six-foot-six-inch wife who weighed 300 pounds, thundered when she walked, and would come sit on us if we acted up. For the record, I loved those stories, but since the days of the monstrous Mrs. Martin I have come to see history sing, dance, and even fly on its own wings, when I can see that the people who shaped the ideas and won the battles were real people like me. History becomes powerful when we see that the main characters were not outdated, dusty saints, but rather modern men and women in their time like we are in ours.

My job has been to bring history close and show it as something that really did happen and really does mean something *for us*. For this reason, I have sought to clear the debris of academic articles, old letters, and 600-page biographies to give you a smooth run down the mountain. The histories in this book are not dry essays or even cradle-to-grave biographies. Instead, they are stories of friendships between real people who thought and spoke much like we do. I have chosen to record dialogue in contemporary English because modern speech helps close the gap between us and history like nothing else.[5] Where possible, I have preserved exact words, using verbatim quotations from letters, journals, and sermons; while in other situations I've filled real historical scenes with dialogue that seems consistent with what I've learned of the personality, beliefs, and circumstances of the characters.

I hope to reclaim our forgotten history and reintroduce it to you in a way that's both accessible and inspiring. I believe that when you and I can imagine ourselves on the inside of history's great movements, then we are on our way to discovering our place in the stories yet to be written.

"Is this book only for the rich?" some have asked. No. God wants to see our faithful stewardship in little or much. Remember Jesus' parable of the talents? The person who originally received five talents and the one who had two talents received equal praise for their good stewardship. They each heard their master say, "Well done, good and faithful servant."[6] The Bible

---

5   My inspiration for this approach comes largely from Dorothy Sayers' approach to retelling the life of Jesus in her series of BBC radio plays *The Man Born To Be King*.

6   Matthew 25:14–23.

tells us that God cares less about how much we have and more about what we do with it.

This message of Gospel Patronage is not something new for a select few, but a focused application of the gospel for all of us. The truth is no matter how much or how little you have been given, there is eternity to think about what you did with it, and hearing Jesus say, "Well done" will be the only thing that matters.

Biblical Patrons

"Yes, but is Gospel Patronage even biblical?" you ask. Good question. Allow me to point out a few examples that for years have been right under our noses— in the Bible.

First, how did Jesus and his disciples fund three years of preaching tours from town to town and village to village after they had all left their jobs? Surely every lunch wasn't a miracle meal of fishes and loaves. The Bible tells us, in Luke 8:1-3, that three generous women named Mary, Joanna, and Susanna came alongside Jesus and the disciples to provide for their ministry:

> Soon afterward he [Jesus] went on through cities and
> villages, proclaiming and bringing the good news of the
> kingdom of God. And the twelve were with Him, and
> also some women who had been healed of evil spirits
> and infirmities: Mary, called Magdalene, from whom
> seven demons had gone out, and Joanna, the wife of

Chuza, Herod's household manager, and Susanna, and
many others, who provided for them out of their means.

These three women who were "with Him" also "provided for them out of their means." They were involved and invested in Jesus' ministry. Jesus Christ had Gospel Patrons.

In the book of Acts we meet Priscilla and Aquila, a married couple in the early church, who were business people. But that did not stop them from engaging in God's business to advance the gospel. They hosted a church in their house, came alongside a well-known preacher named Apollos and helped him with his theology, and partnered with the apostle Paul at the risk of their own lives. (See these stories in Acts 18:1–3, 26 and 1 Cor. 16:19). Priscilla and Aquila may never have addressed a crowd or preached a sermon, but their calling to support the church and spread the gospel earned them the thanks of "all the churches." Paul says: "Greet Priscilla and Aquila, my fellow workers in Christ Jesus, who risked their necks for my life, to whom not only I give thanks but all the churches of the Gentiles give thanks as well."[7]

Interestingly, the only reason we know the story of Priscilla and Aquila 2,000 years later is due to another patron, an influential Greek man mentioned in the opening lines of the books Luke and Acts. In Luke 1:3 we read: "It seemed good to me also, having followed all things closely for some time past, to write an orderly account for you, most excellent Theophilus" and in

---

7   Romans 16:3–4.

Acts 1:1-2 we find: "In the first book, O Theophilus, I have dealt with all that Jesus began to do and teach, until the day when he was taken up."

It is very likely that Luke researched and wrote about Jesus' life and the spread of Christianity because Theophilus funded him to do it.[8] Theophilus could never have imagined at the time that through his patronage of Luke he was underwriting two books of the Bible!

Lastly, a woman named Phoebe used her home to host missionaries as well as the church in her city. She even assisted the apostle Paul and many others with their financial needs. Phoebe's greatest ministry responsibility was likely to hand-carry Paul's letter to the Christians in Rome. For these reasons, Paul described her with the title *patron*: "Welcome her [Phoebe] in the Lord in a way worthy of the saints, and help her in whatever she may need from you, for she has been a patron of many and of myself as well."[9]

The Bible and history confirm that Gospel Patronage is not something new. It's not a fad. Instead it's a flag. This book is my attempt to wave it for a new generation.

---

8 This is one of several interpretations of Theophilus. I am aware of the other views, but I see the patron relationship as the most plausible.

9 Romans 16:2.

gos • pel pa • trons, *noun*. **1.** people who resource and come alongside others to help them proclaim the gospel.

For the word of God is living and active...

2 The English Bible

Tyndale & Monmouth

Humphrey Monmouth leaned back in his chair, looked out over London's overcast skyline, and paused from what he was reading. The news had come from abroad. He already knew what had happened, but somehow he still feared having those grave words pass before his eyes. To avoid the next sentence would not change the truth; he knew that, but he wished it could.

Monmouth took a deep breath and read on: "After sixteen months in Vilvorde Prison, William Tyndale is now dead." Instantly, thoughts of his own imprisonment flooded Monmouth's mind. His arrest, interrogation, and incarceration had all occurred because of his partnership with Tyndale. And now, his good friend William Tyndale was dead at the age of forty-one.

"You did it, William," Monmouth said under his breath. "We did it," he whispered, "and England will never be the same."

With tears glistening on his round face, Monmouth recalled the first time he had met Tyndale, nearly fourteen years earlier, in the spring of 1523.

Plain English

"Good evening, everyone." The man at the front of the church began speaking just as the wealthy London businessman seated himself in the back row. "So that's the man I've heard about," the businessman thought, noting that the speaker was in his late twenties, with a light complexion, high forehead, a strong nose, steady and serious eyes, and a blond beard that hid his slender face.

"Tonight's message comes from the book of Romans," the preacher continued.

"I should meet him afterward," the businessman thought to himself. After the event ended, the businessman stayed behind, waiting until the crowd had thinned out. He finally approached the preacher. "Excuse me, sir."

"Oh, hello. How do you do? I'm William Tyndale." The preacher spoke in the same confident voice that had echoed from the pulpit a few minutes earlier.

"I hear you're from Gloucester?"

"I am, but most recently I've come from the Cotswolds," said Tyndale.

The two men continued making small talk until another well-wisher interrupted.

"You sir, with that Bible open, make each verse an arrow destined for its target," the older gentleman told Tyndale. "Next time I will insist that my wife and brother come to hear you."

"Thank you so much," said Tyndale softly.

The old man started in on a story that showed no signs of ending, something about Parliament's likelihood to pass an anti-French covenant. The businessman drifted away but caught Tyndale's eye with a sympathetic wave before fading out through the front door of the church.

The businessman understood now why people of St. Dunstan-in-the-West appreciated Tyndale so much. They frequently said he took what was fuzzy and frustrating about Christianity and made it clear and compelling—in plain English. "Plain English like a true Englishman," they added for emphasis.

A few weeks later, Tyndale was back in the pulpit and the businessman was back in the pew. Following his message, Tyndale parted the sea of well-wishers and made his way toward the businessman.

"I didn't catch your name last time," he acknowledged.

"I'm Humphrey Monmouth, a cloth merchant on London's eastside."

"Pleasure to meet you. I have a brother in the cloth trade."

"Well then I'm sure you know that England makes the best wool in all of Europe and Cotswold sheep make the best wool in all of England," the merchant boasted.

"That's what they say."

"But, didn't you say you just came from the country? What were you doing there?" Monmouth inquired.

"I tutored John Walsh's two boys at Little Sodbury Manor. They put me up in their spacious attic. I couldn't have asked for better accommodations. That place became a sanctuary for time with the Master."

"I can tell," said the businessman, remembering the old story of common fishermen made bold by their time with the same Master. "How about some steak and a pint of beer?" Monmouth offered. "It'll renew the preacher's strength. My treat."

"I can hardly refuse," said Tyndale.

As they walked, the two men discussed news from home and abroad with occasional dips into the way things are and the way things ought to be. They found a seat in a pub on Fleet Street.

"Your message tonight …" Monmouth began earnestly.

"I know," interrupted the preacher, ready to deflect criticism.

"No, no, I'm not criticizing. Quite the opposite," Monmouth reassured him. "I'm glad there's one preacher in London who keeps me awake. I don't care for most of them, you know. But you teach straight from the Bible. I like that."

"That's the problem," Tyndale said. "Most men know so little of God's word. That's why I'm in London. I want to change that. But just when I thought things were speeding up, they've stopped."

"What do you mean?"

Tyndale pulled a letter from the inside pocket of his jacket. "Read it," he said, passing the letter across the table. "It's from Tunstall."

"Bishop Tunstall? What about?"

Tyndale nodded and pointed to the letter. Monmouth read aloud:

Dear Master Tyndale,
Many thanks for your inquiry and your fine piece of
translation. At this time, my house is full and I have
more guests than I can well look after. Do seek work in

London. I'm sure you will not fail to find the support
you need.

Most sincerely,
C. Tunstall, Bishop of London

"What's he talking about?" Monmouth inquired.

"I sought Bishop Tunstall's patronage." Tyndale's countenance sank, and he sighed before continuing. "I thought he would help me—but full—his house is full."

Monmouth stared intently into his new friend's face. "Go on," he prodded.

"From Oxford to London, from country chapels to city churches, I have seen that men are ignorant of God's word," Tyndale explained. "Latin stifles the faith of our land. Most people know only a few words of it, including the priests. Those who do, use it as a power play to hawk God's grace and fatten their pocketbooks."

"Well? What do you propose?"

"An English New Testament."

"And overturn the Latin?!" Monmouth said in shock.

"The Latin Vulgate has gone unchanged and unchallenged for a thousand years. Tradition after tradition has been built upon it," Tyndale said. "But I've read the New Testament in its original language. The Greek makes clear that some official church practices are based on mistakes. With a Bible in the language of the people, translated from the original Greek, we could steer our whole nation back to Christianity's true core—faith alone in Jesus Christ."

"But what about the Pope and the Constitution prohibiting Bible translation? You could be burned as a heretic!"

"I defy the Pope and all his laws! If God spares my life for many years, I will cause a boy that drives the plough to know more of the Scripture than he does!"

At that the men sat silent, pondering the preacher's words and the strength with which he said them. Common people knew about the Bible, but they did not know the Bible for themselves. They relied on the church to teach them. But the church's Christianity had been reduced to the lowest common denominator, a system of rewards and punishments mingled with vague ideas about God.[1]

Finally Monmouth broke the silence, "Dear Master Tyndale, many thanks for your inquiry and your fine piece of translation. God has given you a job to do, and it's time you get to work. Most sincerely, H. Monmouth, Bishop of Nothing, Patron of One." He sketched his signature in the air.

Tyndale's eyes widened in shock.

"You can lodge in my home," Monmouth said casually, "I have a room upstairs for you. It doesn't have oak beams and all that, but I trust you have an imagination."

"What? I ... ah ..."

"Business always has its risks, Tyndale. Why not add one more to keep life interesting?" he said with a chuckle. The two shook hands. Their partnership had begun.

---

1   Hans J. Hillerbrand, *The World of the Reformation* (Grand Rapids: Baker, 1973), 5.

Table Talk

For the next six months Tyndale worked day and night, translating the Bible into English.[2] Meanwhile, Monmouth entertained a variety of successful merchants, prominent clergymen, and scholars.[3] He was a man of the world, who had traveled and done business abroad, the sort of man who loved to discuss affairs and issues. In the evenings, Tyndale would emerge to dine alongside Monmouth and his guests.

"North Sea's been cold this winter," said an experienced merchant with a husky voice.

"That's your old bones talking," taunted a younger man. "I've made a dozen trips already and ..."

"G'd evenin', Pastor," interrupted the first man, happy that Tyndale's arrival gave him an excuse to change the subject.

"Good evening, men," replied Tyndale as he seated himself with the six merchants who joined his patron at a long wooden table. All were recently returned from voyages, eager for a good English meal and the chance to jostle each other again.

The younger merchant tried to regain control of the conversation, although with a slightly less antagonistic tone. "My trips to Antwerp have been filled with news about Luther," he said. "The Germans rave about him."

"He certainly kicked over the bees' nest," chimed Monmouth.

"And stirred the pot," said the veteran.

---

2 David Daniell, *William Tyndale: A Biography* (New Haven: Yale University Press, 2001), 103; John Foxe, The Acts and Monuments of John Foxe (London: Religious Tract Society, 1563), 4:618.

3 J. F. Mozley, *William Tyndale* (Westport, Conn.: Greenwood Press, 1971), 46.

"You mean turned over the tables," added the younger man.

"I mean Moses had his staff, Samson his donkey's jawbone, David his five smooth stones, and Luther his German Bible," the older merchant thundered.

"So the winds of Germany gust into England then, do they?" Monmouth questioned.

"I've seen copies of his books and pamphlets here in London," another merchant remarked.

Tyndale helped himself to bread and butter, listening intently.

"Pass the meat," ordered Monmouth. He took a second helping and then passed the platter to Tyndale. "A man who's been reading dead languages all day needs meat."

The merchants continued talking of Luther as if they were eyewitnesses called to testify in court.

"Rome is furious with him."

"But the commoners love him alright."

"They say he was raised as a peasant and trained as a priest. That's why he can challenge the church and rally the nation as he does."

"They're reading the Bible in German; how could they not love him?"

"I heard that Luther talked to mothers at home, children in the street, and men in the market. He listened to how they spoke and translated his Bible into language they could understand."

"That's true. He published it just last September."

"Whatever he's done, Europe rumbles under his impact. Sola scriptura and sola fide, they cry."

"And the epicenter," Monmouth noted, "is Wittenberg.

That's Luther's lair."

As the conversation continued, Monmouth noticed Tyndale was silent, and he was pretty sure he knew why. The businessman guessed that Tyndale was wondering if he could do for England what Luther had done for Germany. Monmouth, too, was wondering, what might God do if Tyndale could supply their nation with an English Bible? It was around Monmouth's table that the future of the English Bible unfolded.

After the winter under his patron's roof, it was time for Tyndale to leave the country he loved. Monmouth and the merchants had worked out where he would go, how he would get there, and their plans for a New Testament. They promised to send money for his expenses and connect him with others on the Continent.[4] So in April of 1524, at thirty years of age, William Tyndale bid farewell to his native land; he would never set foot on it again. After a month of travel, Tyndale landed in Wittenberg, Germany.

From Germany

Wittenberg was one of the few places reformers were safe and so it became Europe's hub for men who agreed with Martin Luther. Luther's recently published German Bible made him the perfect advisor for Tyndale's translation project. Within a year the English New Testament was ready to print and Tyndale left Wittenberg for Cologne, one of the three great trading

---

4   Daniell, *William Tyndale*, 108.

ports of northeast Europe, an obvious location to ship books to England.

But outside of Wittenberg Tyndale was no longer safe. Just as his printer neared the end of the Gospel of Matthew, local authorities broke in to arrest him and confiscate his work. Narrowly escaping, Tyndale fled up the Rhine to Worms to begin again. By the early part of the next year, 1526, he had managed to get 3,000 copies of the English New Testament off the presses! But the time for celebrating had not yet come.

These Bibles were considered contraband. God's word in English was illegal. Tyndale again needed Monmouth and the merchants, but this time he needed them to become smugglers. The merchants took these 3,000 volumes and tucked them away in secretly marked crates and hid them in bundles of cloth. Others carefully buried the Bibles in sacks of flour. Still others sealed the Tyndale Bibles in watertight boxes and dropped them in barrels of wine or oil. Some built wooden chests with false sides or secret compartments to perfectly conceal the pocket-sized books.[5]

These first printed copies of the English New Testament were carried across the English Channel, along the international trade routes, into the ports and rivers and creeks of the eastern seaboard, over the hills and wetlands, and up the arteries leading to London. They were sold in bookshops and markets, through private dealers and individual believers. Tailors, farmers, weavers, bricklayers, servants, and apprentices all sought Scripture. One baker paid four shillings for his copy. Another

---

5   Daniell, *William Tyndale*, 186.

man bought two unbound copies for three shillings and four pence. For a little less than that, two men went in together for one.[6] The owners of the forbidden Bibles invited groups of people to meet secretly in their homes so they could listen to God's Word read aloud in English.

This Bible lit the fuse to the English Reformation, and church leaders knew it. As it often is, the issue at stake was the issue of authority. Is tradition, reason, or revelation the highest authority? Tyndale's translation exalted God's revelation, reinstating Scripture as the highest authority. The common people began to see that the doctrine of purgatory was not rooted in the Bible. Neither was the ability to pay for your sins through good works, the purchase of indulgences, or confession to a priest. Fearing they were losing control, the church delivered an official warning:

Many children of iniquity, maintainers of Luther's sect, blinded through extreme wickedness, wandering from the way of truth and the Catholic faith, have craftily translated the New Testament into our English tongue ... seducing common people, attempting by their wicked and perverse interpretations to profane the majesty of Scripture.[7]

---

6   Daniell, *William Tyndale*, 195–96.
7   Daniell, *William Tyndale*, 190.

Tyndale was labeled a heretic, and many of his Bibles were confiscated and burned. On several occasions, the king of England sent emissaries to Europe to urge Tyndale to stop writing and come home. However, Tyndale did not trust the King's promise of protection, especially not after his friend and patron Humphrey Monmouth had been arrested.

A Year in the Tower

The storm that had been swirling around Tyndale and his Bible now swept over Monmouth. Two influential men, Thomas More and William Kingston, raged through Monmouth's house searching for contraband books and correspondence with heretics.[8] Thomas More hated Tyndale. More, a lawyer and a statesman, was offended by the English New Testament.[9] In his view, the church could not possibly be in error; therefore, Tyndale and anyone who helped him should be subdued and punished.[10]

Monmouth was arrested in May of 1528 and indicted on twenty four counts, including:

> *Smuggling Luther's books.*
> *Aiding Tyndale's translation of the English New Testament.*
> *Helping the New Testament be printed and brought into England.*

---

8   John Strype, *Ecclesiastical Memorials* vol. 1, pt. 1 (Clarendon Press, 1822), 488.
9   Daniell, *William Tyndale*, 262.
10 Personal communication with Andrew Hope, member of the Tyndale Society and his unpublished paper "New Research into Humphrey Monmouth" (February 2006), 34.

> *Believing that Christian men should worship God only and
> not saints.*

> *Affirming that salvation is by faith alone, without
> any works.*[11]

Monmouth was taken from his comfortable home and placed
on a barge that carried him down the River Thames, which had
been dyed a rusty brown by the heavy May rain. Floating under London Bridge, he came upon a ghastly sight: the severed
heads of people found guilty of treason that had been impaled
on spikes and left as a warning.[12]

The barge moved toward the intimidating stone fortress
above the river's north bank. Any Londoner could identify
the tower whose silhouette had dominated the skyline since
the eleventh century. As they neared the Traitor's Gate, a water entrance opened, and swallowed the barge whole. They
crossed the forty meter moat and stepped off the barge inside
the ten foot thick defensive walls. Guards marched Monmouth
through a dark, damp, cold, stone hallway. Cell doors opened
and quickly shut behind him. Humphrey Monmouth, a wealthy
businessman and devoted Christian, was seeing the Tower of
London from the inside.

Monmouth sat in the silence, contemplating his situation.
Here he was, barred from society, detained in the most forti-
fied fortress in England, and uncertain of his future. One in ten

---

11   Daniell, *William Tyndale*, 102–3; Strype, *Ecclesiastical Memorials*, 1.1:489.
12   "The Tower of London," English Monarchs website, http://www.englishmonarchs.co.uk/
       tower_london_2.htm.

prisoners was executed inside. Would he be the one? He had a wife and two young daughters, Elizabeth and Grace. What would happen to them? Had he been a fool to support Tyndale? Monmouth could have pitied himself. He could have recanted. Instead, he chose to set his sharp and strategic mind to work crafting a petition for his release. He noted how his absence compounded England's pain of large scale unemployment, since many people depended on Monmouth for work.[13] The businessman also pointed out how his inability to buy and sell cloth from inside the Tower further tightened an already stretched market. On these grounds, he appealed to Cardinal Wolsey, the man most likely to feel the public backlash of these economic troubles.

Initially, Monmouth's petition fell flat. Summer came and went in the Tower. Then fall. Then a cold Christmas ... alone. Winter rolled into spring. Finally, after twelve months inside, Monmouth was released. He had lost a year, but his faith had led him through the fire, and he emerged on the other side unscathed. Still, he couldn't help but wonder what would become of his exiled friend, William Tyndale.

Betrayal and Faith

As Humphrey Monmouth re-entered his life, Tyndale remained in Belgium, at peace among the English merchants in Antwerp. He continued revisions on his New Testament, which by now had gone through five print runs. He also began the translation

---

13   Hope, *New Research*, 32.

of an English Old Testament from the original Hebrew, determined to finish a complete English Bible.[14] Although far away from Monmouth's table, Tyndale still dined with merchants. One of them was an intelligent man named Henry Phillips. One afternoon Phillips invited Tyndale to dinner.

"No, I have plans to go out for dinner tonight," said Tyndale. "But come with me and you will be my guest."

Phillips agreed. "I'll come by later on so we can go together."

When the time came, the two proceeded to leave Tyndale's house through a long and narrow entry, wide enough for only one man at a time. Phillips insisted that Tyndale go first and as they exited the passageway, Phillips raised his arm and pointed down at Tyndale's head to the two officers he had stationed outside. The men pounced on their prey, carrying Tyndale off to Vilvorde Prison.[15] Tyndale, like his Savior, had been betrayed.

The English merchants in Antwerp were outraged and wrote hurriedly to the Court at Brussels as well as the English government seeking Tyndale's release.[16] But there was no response. Tyndale was charged with heresy, just as his patron had been and now suffered in prison for sixteen months, 450 days. But these days were anything but wasted. Tyndale wrote letters and kept working on his translation. His only surviving letter from prison tells us much about the man he was. It was a letter to his prison warden and it reads:

---

14   Daniell, *William Tyndale*, 187–88, 361.
15   Daniell, *William Tyndale*, 364.
16   Daniell, *William Tyndale*, 366.

I believe that you are not unaware of what may have been determined concerning me. Wherefore I beg your lordship, and that by the Lord Jesus, that if I am to remain here through the winter, you will request the commissary to have the kindness to send me, from my goods that he has, a warmer cap; for I suffer greatly from cold in the head, and am afflicted by a perpetual cold, which is much increased in this cell; a warmer coat also, for this which I have is very thin; a piece of cloth too to patch my leggings. My overcoat is worn out; my shirts are also worn out. He has a woolen shirt, if he will be good enough to send it. I have also with him leggings of thicker cloth to put on above; he has also warmer night-caps. And I ask to be allowed to have a lamp in the evening; it is indeed wearisome sitting alone in the dark. But most of all I beg and beseech your clemency to be urgent with the commissary, that he will kindly permit me to have the Hebrew Bible, Hebrew grammar, and Hebrew dictionary, that I may pass the time in that study. In return may you obtain what you most desire, so only that it be for the salvation of your soul. But if any other decision has been taken

concerning me, to be carried out before winter, I will be
patient, abiding the will of God, to the glory of the grace
of my Lord Jesus Christ: whose Spirit, I pray, may ever
direct your heart. Amen.

W. Tyndale[17]

Whether his requests were granted or not is unknown. But what is known is that Tyndale sat alone, in the dark, concerned to finish an English Old Testament and complete the work God had given him to do. Successions of priests and monks were sent to argue with him and get him to recant. And although isolated, in poor health, and with no earthly comforts, Tyndale's faith did not fail. He was willing to give his life to defend the doctrine at the heart of the gospel—justification by faith.[18] And so he would.

On an October morning in 1536, a barricade held the large crowd at a distance. Inside the circular space were a few chairs and a great wood beam. As if on cue, the crowd parted for the guards and their prisoner. Tyndale paused to offer a silent prayer heavenward. Placing his back against the beam, the guards secured Tyndale's feet and his chest with iron chains.[19] A rough rope was wrapped around his neck. As he felt the pressure against his throat, Tyndale glanced at the nearby heap of

17   Daniell, *William Tyndale*, 379. (I omitted "right worshipful" and "catarrh").

18   Daniell, *William Tyndale*, 262, 377.

19   John Foxe includes a woodcut of Tyndale's execution in his Acts & Monuments. See John Foxe's The Acts and Monuments Online: www.johnfoxe.org.

brushwood, logs, and straw that would soon be packed tightly around him, scraping his legs.

The executioner moved behind the beam, and the chief prosecutor and his colleagues sat down in chairs facing Tyndale. Knowing this was his last moment, Tyndale roared in a loud voice, "Lord! Open the King of England's eyes!"[20]

Just then, the chief prosecutor signaled the executioner. The noose was pulled tight; Tyndale was strangled to death. A lighted wax torch lit the flame that burned his body. All that remained was the echo of Tyndale's prayer for his king.

A Prayer Answered

In his London home, Humphrey Monmouth read again the words describing his friend's death. Even through his sadness, Monmouth felt a sense of pride. "You did it, William," Monmouth said under his breath. "We did it," he whispered, "and England will never be the same."

Humphrey Monmouth would live less than a year after his friend Tyndale; it was as if his mission was now complete as well. What the partnership between Monmouth and Tyndale launched was nothing less than a reformation. After the common people gained an appetite for the Scriptures, translations of the English Bible could not be stopped. Men like Miles Coverdale and John Rogers picked up where Tyndale left off, finishing the Old Testament and printing complete English Bibles.

Within two years, God answered Tyndale's prayer. The King

---

20   Daniell, *William Tyndale*, 262, 383.

of England's eyes were opened, and in 1538 he ordered that every parish church should receive its own copy of the English Bible.[21] The plough boy got his Scripture, and so did the other six million Englishmen.[22]

Seventy five years after Tyndale's death, King James authorized an updated English translation. The team of translators relied heavily on Tyndale's work, carrying over eighty to ninety percent into this new Authorized Version.[23] The King James Bible went on to become the most influential book in the English-speaking world. It accompanied English and American citizens in their travels around the world. Over the next 450 years it held sway as the primary English Bible in families, schools, and churches. History, language, and culture have all been shaped by this book. It is found in George Washington's addresses, Abraham Lincoln's speeches, Charles Spurgeon's preaching, Billy Graham's sermons, Winston Churchill's speeches, and Martin Luther King's famous "I Have a Dream" speech.[24]

The flame lit in Tyndale and Monmouth's generation still burns in ours. Every English translation of the Bible finds its headwaters at Tyndale's spring.[25] Today, there are more than six hundred million English speakers who directly benefit from William Tyndale's life and work.[26] History remembers Tyndale,

21 Gerald Bray, *Translating the Bible: From William Tyndale to King James* (London: Latimer Trust, 2010), 9.

22 Daniell, *William Tyndale*, 142.

23 Leland Ryken, *The Legacy of the King James Bible* (Wheaton, Ill.: Crossway, 2011), 29; Bray, Translating the Bible, 8.

24 Ryken, *Legacy*, 101-4.

25 Ryken, *Legacy*, 27.

26 David Daniell, ed., *Tyndale's New Testament* (New Haven, Conn.:Yale University Press), vii.

but it has largely forgotten that behind this massive movement of God was a businessman. In the shadows of the English Reformation stands an invaluable Gospel Patron named Humphrey Monmouth.

I commend to you our sister Phoebe, a servant
of the church at Cenchreae, ... for she has been a
patron of many and of myself as well.

ROMANS 16:1-2

3 The 18th-Century Revival

Whitefield & Lady Huntingdon

Two hundred years after Tyndale and Monmouth, the English Bibles that those men had given their lives to produce now sat in homes and churches collecting dust. Deism was the religion of the day, and most people ignored the Bible's teaching on sin, salvation, and a coming day of judgment. Church was stuffy and formal, and its ministers were timid Mr. Collins-types, who attracted and inspired no one. As a result, society was out of control.

This is how the eighteenth-century began. But by God's grace, this is not how it would end. In His mercy, God united a passionate preacher and a single-minded patroness to spread the gospel far and wide. Their two minds met for this single purpose. Their two paths joined to make a wide road. The turning points of their lives became the turning point in a revival that woke up their nation to God.

A Lady of Rare Qualities

The knock on the door roused the doorman of a London mansion. Guests were not expected, but visitors were not unusual either. The poor came by day to visit Lady Huntingdon's kitchen, and the rich circled round at night to enjoy her parties. But this knock brought her favorite kind of visitor.

"Excuse me, sir," said a tired voice. "Is this the home of Lady Huntingdon?"

"Yes," said the doorman.

"Might I have a word with her, sir?"

"Does she know you?"

"No. But I've walked miles to beg her assistance. You see, my village has no gospel preacher, and I had hoped her Ladyship might send one of her Methodist ministers over and help us."[1]
This poor man had come to the home of a woman who was a tornado and a silver spoon wrapped into one, a 5'6" force of nature and the heiress of old money. Blunt, opinionated, and constantly in motion, Lady Huntingdon was a rare English aristocrat. She rubbed shoulders with royalty, enjoyed a pinch of snuff, and really believed the Bible.

Lady Huntingdon greeted her guest warmly and heard his request. Eventually, the man asked, "Is it true, Madam, that George Whitefield is one of your chaplains?"

"Yes," she answered simply.

"Well then, thank you, thank you, thank you, Madam, for all you've done for England."

A Nation Asleep

Years before Lady Huntingdon received this visitor, she sat by a fire on a wintry night writing letters.

"To John Wesley, my dear friend," she scribbled. "As we came into the town of Gloucester, we met on horseback, coming out

---

1   Faith Cook, *Selina: Countess of Huntingdon* (Carlisle, Pa.: Banner of Truth, 2001), 334.

of the town Mr. Whitefield who stopped to tell me he would be back by eight o'clock and would then wait upon me—."[2] While she was writing, a knock came at the door.

"Good evening, Lady Huntingdon," said a strong and melodious voice. Her guest was a slender man in his late twenties, of average height, with a pale and cheerful face.

"Welcome back," she responded. He sat down and was promptly poured a cup of tea.

"Mr. Whitefield, it's been a long time since I last heard you preach in London," Lady Huntingdon said.

"Nearly three years, I believe. Just before I sailed to Philadelphia."

"And how did you like the colonies?"

"Very well. I believe America is to be my chief scene for action."[3]

"I read in the papers about your marriage to Elizabeth James."

"Yes, Elizabeth plans to join my next trip to America and work with the Orphan House. But I'm curious, Madam, what brings you to Gloucester in the middle of winter?"

"My friends and I return from Bath because my doctor advised me to take the waters of Bath, but the city itself is enough to make me sick all over again. In my opinion, it is a silly playground for the rich—the most stupid place I've ever seen.[4] Endless entertainment, drinking, and gambling ... vanity of

2   John R. Tyson and Boyd S. Schlenther, *In the Midst of Early Methodism* (Scarecrow Press, 2006), 49–50.
3   John Pollock, *George Whitefield and the Great Awakening* (Chariot Victor, 1986), 167.
4   Tyson and Schlenther, *Midst*, 24.

vanities! Worst of all," she said angrily, "they find our doctrine repulsive. The Duchess of Buckingham wrote me the following line and I quote:

> *It is monstrous to be told that you have a heart as sinful as the common wretches that crawl on the earth. This is highly offensive and insulting to those of us with high rank and good breeding.*[5]

"What pride the rich have, Mr. Whitefield. I am quite out of patience at the wickedness of them all."[6]

"The love of money ..."

"Exactly," interrupted the Countess passionately.

"...is the reason many are no more than almost Christians. I wish the Church of England was the joy of the whole earth, but the Christian world is instead in a deep sleep."[7]

"Whitefield, I am sure more vileness and wickedness never abounded in the Christian Church as it does now."[8]

After Whitefield left, the Countess sat quietly, her head slouched into her hand and her eyes downcast. The weight of her nation's sinful condition seemed to double gravity's downward pull. In cities like Bath, parties, fashion shows, concerts, and gambling houses intoxicated the rich for months at a time.

---

5   Cook, *Selina*, 69.
6   Tyson and Schlenther, *Midst*, 25.
7   Arnold A. Dallimore, *George Whitefield: The Life and Times of the Great Evangelist of the Eighteenth-Century Revival* (Carlisle, Pa.: Banner of Truth, 1970), 1:339, 252; George Whitefield, "The Almost Christian" *Selected Sermons of George Whitefield*, http://www.ccel.org/ccel/whitefield/sermons.html.
8   Tyson and Schlenther, *Midst*, 83.

They sat down to eat and drink and rose up to play with no thought of eternity.[9]

"But Lord, what am I to do about it?" she prayed. "My generation lies lost in darkness. They're like sheep without a shepherd. God, may you pour abundant blessings upon our sinful country and help me to fill my place in your work?"[10]

A Skeleton in Bed

Over the next few years, Lady Huntingdon was fully engaged as a wife and mother. She had a happy marriage. She and her husband traveled together, went to church together, and socialized among the highest society in England. Lady Huntingdon doted on her husband, calling him "my dear jewel" and "my angel" and writing to him notes such as, "God has so uncommonly blessed us here on earth together" again "So absolutely are you the object of all my earthly pleasure."[11]

But one morning over breakfast, Lord Huntingdon said to his wife, "I had the most alarming dream last night."

"What was it, my dearest?"

"A skeleton stood at the foot of our bed. And after standing a while, it untucked the sheets and crept up underneath them to the top of our bed—and lay between us."[12]

"Chilling," she said with a shiver. "What do you think it means?"

9   Exodus 32:6.
10 Cook, *Selina*, 103.
11 Tyson and Schlenther, *Midst*, 5, 23, 24, 33.
12 Cook, *Selina*, 98.

"I believe the skeleton was ..." He paused.

"Was what?" she demanded.

"Death."

Their conversation stopped. They solemnly stared into each other's eyes. There was nothing to say. And within two weeks, Lord Huntingdon died of a stroke.[13]

For months Lady Huntingdon withdrew from society, grieving at her husband's graveside. At thirty-nine years old, with four children to care for, and vast estates to look after, Lady Huntingdon was a widow. The loss of her husband became one of the greatest turning points of her life.

Not a Velvet-Mouthed Preacher

Meanwhile, Whitefield had been back and forth to America several times and had seen God work through him to awaken thousands to faith in Jesus Christ. He had begun preaching just months after his conversion when he was a twenty-one-year-old Oxford student. Unlike the sedate preachers all around him, Whitefield was a man on fire.

At a time when most sermons were dry, moral essays read from church pulpits, Whitefield's words were like living water overflowing from his heart. The Bible's truths of heaven and hell, God and Satan, sin and salvation, were all realities to Whitefield, and he preached them that way.[14]

---

13 Cook, *Selina*, 98.
14 Lady Huntingdon wrote, "He appeared to speak of spiritual and divine things as awful realities." Aaron Seymour, *The Life and Times of Selina, Countess of Huntingdon* (London: W.E. Painter, 1844), 1:163.

"I'll tell you a story," Whitefield offered in the middle of one of his sermons:

In the year 1675 the Archbishop of Canterbury was acquainted with an actor named Mr. Butterton. One day the Archbishop said to Butterton, "Tell me, Mr. Butterton, what is the reason you actors on stage can affect your congregations with speaking of things imaginary, as if they were real, while we in church speak of things real, which our congregations only receive as if they were imaginary?" "Why, my Lord," says Butterton, "the reason is very plain. We actors on stage speak of things imaginary as if they were real and you in the pulpit speak of things real as if they were imaginary."

At the end of this story, Whitefield shouted loudly, "Therefore, I will not be a velvet-mouthed preacher."[15]

George Whitefield was thunder and lightning, a man made to awaken the slumbering. He spoke in a way that showed spiritual things to be real. He was biblical, passionate, dramatic, and joyful. He loved the people he preached to, frequently wept in his sermons, and urgently pleaded with everyone to come to Jesus. Whitefield's maxim was: "to preach, as Apelles painted, for eternity."[16] He often said, "Would ministers preach for eternity, they would then act the part of true Christian orators, and not

---

15 Harry Stout, *Divine Dramatist* (Grand Rapids: Eerdmans, 1991), 239–40. (I have slightly modernized the language to make it more readable.)

16 Seymour, *Life and Times of Selina*, 2:129.

only calmly and coolly inform the understanding, but by persuasive, passionate address, endeavor to move the affections and warm the heart."[17]

He often preached twice a day seven days a week ... sometimes more. The crowds who came to hear him were so large that he pioneered something no other Englishman had tried— he preached outside. Many who would never enter a church came to hear him in fields, parks, hillsides, and even fairs. When Whitefield came to town, mechanics closed their shops and construction workers left their job sites just to hear him. When he preached at 5 a.m., people came.[18] When his sermons lasted two hours, people stayed.

Sarah Edwards reported on the phenomenon that was George Whitefield:

> *He is truly a remarkable man, and during his visit, has I think verified all we have heard of him. He makes less of the doctrines than our American preachers generally do and aims more at affecting the heart. He is a born orator. You have already heard of his deep-toned yet clear and melodious voice. It is perfect music.*
>
> *It is wonderful to see what a spell he casts over an audience by proclaiming the simplest truths of the Bible. I have seen upwards of a thousand people hang*

17 Seymour, *Life and Times of Selina*, 2:129. (I have updated Whitefield's "pathetic" to "passionate" because by pathetic he meant to move and affect the feelings, which is not the way we use the word today.)

18 Pollock, *George Whitefield*, 164.

on his words with breathless silence, broken only by an occasional half-suppressed sob.

He impresses the ignorant, and not less, the educated and refined ... A prejudiced person, I know might say that this is all theatrical artifice and display; but not so will anyone think who has seen and known him. He is a very devout and godly man, and his only aim seems to be to reach and influence men the best way. He speaks from a heart aglow with love, and pours out a torrent of eloquence which is almost irresistible.[19]

Taking the Word to the Influential

"Mr. Whitefield," called the postman, "welcome back to England, sir. I have a letter for you from Lady Huntingdon."

The preacher thanked him and quickly opened the envelope. It had been six years since his chance meeting with Lady Huntingdon in Gloucester, but he certainly hadn't forgotten her.

"Good Lady Huntington," Whitefield said to himself with a jovial chuckle. "Few women are so fierce and charming. What is she up to now?"

Whitefield read the letter, then hurriedly penned a reply and handed it to the postman. A few days later, he arrived at Lady Huntingdon's London home, where she greeted him warmly.

"Mr. Whitefield, thank you for coming."

"Madam, the honor is mine. How are you?"

---

19 Dallimore, *George Whitefield*, 1:538–39.

"So much has happened since we last met," she said with a sigh. "Two of my sons died of smallpox ..."

"Oh, Madam."

"... and my dearest husband was taken by a stroke."

"I'm terribly sorry."

"As am I, Mr. Whitefield," said the countess. "But amidst my losses, my Savior has heard and answered my prayers. I recently accompanied Howell Harris and three other evangelists on a preaching tour of Wales. Four or five times a day people from little hamlets and villages came to hear the word of God. And God displayed His power in a way I've never seen. During the preaching I walked amidst the crowds and saw how God's word convicted them. With my own eyes I observed their tears, and with my own ears I heard their cries for God's mercy.

"Mr. Whitefield, I watched God save souls through the light of his all-glorious gospel, and now I see the one thing worth living for must be the proclaiming of the love of God to man in Jesus Christ. I am nothing—Christ is all. To behold the glory of such a Savior ought to make us breathe his praises from pole to pole. To preach Christ and his blessing upon repentance over the earth is the commission."[20]

Whitefield sat still.

"So," she said, "My mind is made up. I'd like to propose a partnership."

"Go on," he said.

"God chose me to be a member of England's nobility, and

---

20 Tyson and Schlenther, *Midst*, 181--82 [No. 242: To Philip Doddridge]

now I'm ready to use my position for Jesus' sake. And I want your help."

"I'm listening," Whitefield said, a warm smile spreading across his face like a sunrise.

"Well, Galatians 2:2 says that Paul preached privately to those who seemed influential in Jerusalem.[21] And I have a burden for the influential in England. They won't go out to the fields to hear Methodist preachers, and when they attend church they hear sermons with no theological guts. Whitefield, I want you to bring the gospel to them ... in my home ... starting tomorrow night."

Whitefield was thrilled to answer Lady Huntingdon's call and later wrote to her: "If they will hear the gospel only under a ceiled roof, ministers shall be sent to them there. If only in a church, or a field, they shall have it there. O that I may be enabled, when called to preach to any of them, so to preach as to win their souls to the blessed Jesus!"[22]

A Surprising Introduction

The next night, prominent politicians, actors, writers, lords and ladies, even a few members of the royalty crowded into Lady Huntingdon's drawing room. The women squeezed their wide-hooped skirts through doorways as they balanced tall arrangements of false curls and ornamental flowers atop their heads. The men wore powdered wigs, and the officers in the crowd showed off their dress uniforms, complete with their swords.

---

21 Tyson and Schlenther, *Midst*, 73, see also 20n82.
22 Tyson and Schlenther, *Midst*, 73.

Servants circulated with trays of tea and lemonade.[23]

From the kitchen, a young servant girl wondered dreamily, "What do you think it's like to be a countess?"

"Shh," hushed a slightly older woman.

"What?"

"In your day-dreaming you're clanging those dishes. Just wash 'em. I want it to be quiet for Lady Huntingdon's guests. Besides," she went on in a whisper, "I heard the Prince of Wales and a few members of Parliament will be out there tonight."

"And his Majesty's half-sister, Lady Chesterfield, is coming too," the girl added.

"Shh ...that's the countess's voice!" The party chatter had died out. The women stopped working and pressed their ears against the door.

"Ladies and gentlemen of London, welcome," said Lady Huntingdon. "Tonight I'd like to introduce you to a friend of mine. Many of you are familiar with his name and his reputation, but I'm eager for you to hear from him yourselves. Having just returned from America, he has agreed to speak to us tonight. Please welcome, George Whitefield!"

Whitefield, dressed in his white wig and clergyman's black gown, humbly stepped forward. Without any notes to rely on, the thirty-three-year-old minister opened his Bible and preached a simple, clear, and powerful message. He made it plain to the crowd that "My only aim is to bring you to Christ, to deliver you from your false confidences, to raise you from

---

23   Cook, *Selina*, 117–18.

your dead formality, and to revive real Christianity!"[24] Though Whitefield was in the presence of society's greats, he held nothing back:

> Jesus said it is easier for a camel to go through the eye of a needle than for a rich man to enter into the kingdom of God. Yet even to you that are rich do I now freely offer salvation by Jesus Christ, if you will renounce yourselves and come to Jesus Christ as poor sinners. I say poor sinners for the "poor in spirit" are only so blessed as to have a right to the kingdom of God. And Jesus Christ calls none to Him, but those who thirst after his righteousness and feel themselves weary and heavy laden with the burden of their sins. Consider that Jesus Christ has had mercy on such a wretch as I am, and the same grace which was sufficient for me, is sufficient for you also if you will believe in Jesus Christ whom God has sent. Indeed, you can never believe in or serve a better master, one that is more mighty or more willing to save. Come then, my guilty brothers, come and believe in the Lord that bought you with His precious blood.[25]

---

24 Pollock, *George Whitefield*, 120. (Whitefield used the term "primitive Christianity," but to modern ears primitive does not have the ring of old and true, but simplistic, basic, and elementary. "Real Christianity" is closer to Whitefield's meaning.)

25 Whitefield, "The Indwelling of the Spirit, the Common Privilege of All Believers," *Selected Sermons*.

Whitefield's passionate message erased any indifference
his hearers might have felt. Lady Huntingdon's guests were
so taken with Whitefield that they asked him to preach again.
Two of England's most prominent and yet least religious men
were impressed.

"Mr. Whitefield," said the Earl of Chesterfield, "Sir, I greatly
approve of your preaching."

"Greatly approve?" interrupted Lord Bolingbroke. "Ah Chesterfield, Whitefield here is the most extraordinary man of our
times." Turning to the preacher he added, "Sir, you have the
most commanding eloquence I have ever heard."[26]

"Thank you," Whitefield said. "But more importantly" he re-
directed, "here comes our hostess, a woman who is all aflame
for Jesus."[27]

The countess approached, dressed in an elegant evening
gown of ocean-blue French silk.

"Gentlemen," she said, "I see you've made Mr. Whitefield's
acquaintance. Please allow me to excuse him; there are a few
others who have asked for an introduction."

Later that night after the crowd faded away, Whitefield wrote
to a friend:

I went home never more surprised at any incident in
my life. The prospect of doing good to the rich that
attend her Ladyship's house is very encouraging. Who
knows what God may do? He could never use a more

26   Cook, *Selina*, 110–11.
27   Cook, *Selina*, 115.

insignificant instrument. I want humility, I want
thankfulness, I want a heart continually flaming with
the love of God. Oh pray that God would always keep
me humble and fully convinced that I am nothing with-
out Him, and that all the good which is done upon the
earth is God's doing.[28]

Making a Dream Come True

The prospect of God working powerfully among the rich and
famous thrilled Lady Huntingdon, and she said so in a letter to
her friend Dr. Doddridge:

> *I must tell you, I have had two large assemblies at my*
> *house of the mighty, the humble, the wise and the rich*
> *to hear the gospel by Mr. Whitefield, and I have great*
> *hope for Lord Chesterfield and Lord Bath, Mr. Stan-*
> *hope and one of the privy Council of Denmark, with a*
> *great many ladies and people of fashion. I know your*
> *warm heart will rejoice at this, and your prayers will*
> *help with ours for increase to our Blessed Lord's King-*
> *dom even among these.*[29]

Whitefield was excited too, and he shared the news with one
of his friends, who was also one of America's founding fathers.
Benjamin Franklin wrote the following in reply.

---

28 Luke Tyerman, *The Life of the Reverend George Whitefield* (New York: Anson D. F.
    Randolph, 1877), 2:243, 247; Pollock, *George Whitefield*, 39.
29 Tyson and Schlenther, *Midst*, 73–74.

I am glad to hear that you have frequent opportunities of preaching among the great. If you can gain them to a good and exemplary life, wonderful changes will follow in the manners of the lower ranks. ... On this principle, Confucius, the famous eastern reformer proceeded. ... The mode has a wonderful influence on mankind; and there are numbers, who, perhaps fear less the being in hell, than out of fashion.

Our more western reformation began with the ignorant mob; and when numbers of them were gained, interest and party views drew in the wise and great. Where both methods can be used, reformations are likely to be more speedy. O that some method could be found to make them lasting! He who discovers that, will, in my opinion, deserve more, ten thousand times, than the inventor of longitude.

My wife and family join in the most cordial salutations to you and good Mrs. Whitefield. I am, dear sir,

Your very affectionate friend and

most obliged humble servant,

Benjamin Franklin[30]

Despite Franklin's differing religious views, his theory of "both methods"—winning both the influential and the mob— was key for Whitefield. The common people had initially been

---

30   Dallimore, *George Whitefield*, 2:444.

the only ones to accept the Methodist preachers, but now Whitefield preached in Lady Huntingdon's house each Tuesday and Thursday he was in London. Her unashamed support for Whitefield began a chain reaction. Those who had previously despised the Methodists started to speak of them with a newfound respect; how could they not when a woman as elevated as Lady Huntingdon respected them?[31]

But upon his return from America, Whitefield was under pressure to curb his extraordinary evangelistic efforts, settle down in England, and oversee a denomination of Calvinistic Methodists. People in London offered him large sums of money to stay and preach to them in England; people in Boston, Philadelphia, and Maryland did same. But Whitefield said, "The sight of so many perishing souls every day affects me much, and makes me long to go if possible from pole to pole, to proclaim redeeming love."[32] Lady Huntingdon's patronage made it possible for Whitefield to fulfill this dream.

She asked Whitefield to become one of her personal chaplains, a special privilege reserved for the nobility. Lady Huntingdon's support gave Whitefield the means and the encouragement to continue preaching everywhere, promoting the revival among all churches, all denominations, and all peoples.[33] In a letter to his patroness, Whitefield wrote:

31 Cook, *Selina*, 128.
32 Dallimore, *George Whitefield*, 1:111; 2:207, 220–21.
33 Seymour, *Life and Times of Selina*, 1:93, 183.

*About two thousand attend every night. Last Sunday
evening, in the field, there were about five thousand
hearers. I hear much good has been done at Bristol.
Everywhere, fresh doors are opening, and people
flock from all quarters. I have not been so well for so
long a season for many years as I have been since I left
London; a proof, I think, that the Lord calls me into
the fields.*[34]

No Easy Roads

The preacher kept preaching, and the crowds kept coming,
but not everyone was enthralled with Whitefield's enthusiasm. Opposition met him and this young movement at every
turn. Whitefield preached with tremendous force, and likewise,
those who opposed him did so violently. While he preached
in the fields, he was regularly under fire from rocks, dirt, and
even eggs.[35]

He described one such incident in a letter to Lady
Huntingdon:

*Honored Madam,
I preached twice at Exeter, and in the evening I believe
I had near ten thousand hearers. All was quiet and
there was a great solemnity in the congregation, but
a drunken man threw three great stones at me. One of*

---

34   Tyerman, *Life of the Reverend George Whitefield*, 2:252.
35   Dallimore, *George Whitefield*, 2:118, 397.

them cut my head deeply and was likely to knock me
off the platform, but blessed be God, I did not lose my
composure at all. [36]

On another night, Whitefield set up his pulpit at a seedy fair amidst gambling booths, gin shops, and bare-fisted street-fighters, who supplied the crowd with cheap entertainment. Whitefield's wife, Elizabeth, stood behind him as he began preaching. But Whitefield's courage sank when he saw the hairy-chested bruisers storming in his direction, angry that he had diverted their customers. Just then, he felt a tug on his clothes. It was Elizabeth. "George," she called, "Play the Man for God!" Instantly, Whitefield's courage and compassion surged, and the preacher loudly proclaimed, "I am not ashamed of the Gospel of Christ, for it is the power of God unto salvation to everyone that believes!"[37]

Opposition was common for Whitefield. A mob in Ireland stoned him almost to death; two attackers in Plymouth tried to kill him in his bed one night; and rioters often did whatever they could to distract the preacher and his hearers. But Whitefield would not be silenced. He traveled from town to town, preaching, preaching, always preaching.

Sharing Good News by the Sea

Meanwhile, Lady Huntingdon was facing her own trials. Her younger son, Henry, now fifteen, was slowly going blind from

---

36   Tyerman, *Life of the Reverend George Whitefield*, 2:270.
37   Pollock, *George Whitefield*, 199.

a mysterious disorder.[38] London doctors couldn't fix him, but they recommended a new natural cure: sea bathing. The seaside town of Brighton, fifty miles south of London, was up and coming as a health resort destination, so Lady Huntingdon and her son set out in their carriage across the rough English roads. Arriving in Brighton, the countess was startled to hear a woman call out from the street, "Oh Madam, you have come."

Lady Huntingdon's eyes darted around the busy streets, looking for a face to match with the voice. Seeing a small country woman looking at her, she asked hesitantly, "Do you know me?"

"Madam, I saw you in a dream three years ago," said the woman. "A tall woman dressed as you are now would come to Brighton and she would do us much good here."

Lady Huntingdon visited the woman and discovered she only had a few months to live. But God had graciously prepared the dying woman to hear the gospel and be saved. Lady Huntingdon also learned of a soldier's wife who was not expected to live long after giving birth to twins. Lady Huntingdon shared with her from the Bible about the reality of her sin, and this new mother wept, begging her to return and teach from the Scriptures again.

The bedridden woman's house shared a wall with the public bakehouse, where most people in those days went to bake their bread.[39] Although Lady Huntingdon did not know it, a crack in

---

38 Cook, *Selina*, 174–80. (I'm indebted entirely to Faith Cook's wonderful biography for the following narrative.)

39 Cook, *Selina*, 176.

the wall meant that people standing in line for the oven were overhearing her Bible studies. Word spread around town about a tall woman from London who spoke of the way of forgiveness for sin. Before long, the bedside Bible study grew until it became the core group of a church-plant in Brighton.[40]

Sadly, Henry's condition persisted, and he died three years later, at the age of eighteen. This was another great loss for a woman who had already suffered many and had more to come. Before Lady Huntingdon would pass away, five of her seven children would die. She was a woman who experienced great losses, but through her faith remained strong. And at the age of fifty, one of her biggest victories was still to come.

Transforming a City

All over England, Whitefield's followers formed Societies and began meeting together.[41] What was to be done for all the people who had been saved? Many who had gathered in Lady Huntingdon's home now needed spiritual leadership, a community of like-minded believers, and a place to gather. And who would evangelize England when Whitefield was away in America? These questions captured Lady Huntingdon's attention for the rest of her life.

After thirty years, she returned to Bath, the city that had appalled her when she was younger. This time she bought a plot

---

40 Cook, *Selina*, 179.
41 Dallimore, *George Whitefield*, 2:153. (Dallimore says, "Here then, were thirty-six societies and twenty-five preaching places that sprang up under Whitefield's ministry in the three or four years that followed his return from America in 1741.")

of land, hired builders, and began construction. Lady Huntingdon's project caught the city's attention.

"Why build a chapel?" they questioned. "Your money could
be better spent helping the poor."

"I do pity the poor" she answered, "and I will give them what
I can. But when I gave myself up to the Lord, I likewise devoted
all my fortune to Him with this condition: that I would take with
a sparing hand what might be necessary for my food, clothing,
and support of my children. Many benevolent persons who
have no religion feel for the physical needs of others and help
them. But few, even among professing Christians, have a proper
concern for the awful condition of perishing souls."[42]

With this concern for "perishing souls," Lady Huntingdon
built her chapel in a style that would make the aristocratic resi-
dents of Bath comfortable to enter.[43] Opening day was rainy and
gray, but still the curious crowds of Bath found their way to the
chapel.[44] Whitefield, who was now fifty, ascended the pulpit to
preach to a packed house.

There are a great many who bear the name of Christ,
but do not know what real Christianity is.[45] *I am*
persuaded that the majority of preachers talk of an
unknown and unfelt Christ. The only way to restore the
church to its dignity is to live and preach the doctrine of

42   Seymour, *Life and Times of Selina*, 1:315–16.
43   Cook, *Selina*, 222.
44   Seymour, *Life and Times of Selina*, 1:468.
45   Whitefield, "Marks of a True Conversion," *Selected Sermons*.

Christian.[46] *When you have once tasted of His love and felt
the power of His grace upon your hearts, you will then
love to talk of Jesus.*[47]

Whitefield ended his sermon with a passionate invitation for
his hearers to believe in Jesus:

*O, let there be joy in heaven over some of you who be-
lieve. Let me not go back to my Master and say, "Lord,
they will not believe my report." No longer harden your
hearts, but open them wide, and let the King of glory
enter in. Believe me, I am willing to go to prison or
death for you; but I am not willing to go to heaven without you. The love of Jesus Christ constrains me to lift up
my voice like a trumpet.*[48]

Now at last, Bath had a stage for the truth. Lady Huntingdon
put out urgent messages, soliciting England's best preachers to
come to Bath and continue the momentum begun by Whitefield. By the mercy of God and because of the efforts of the
countess, it became fashionable, in the city widely recognized
for immorality, to meet up with friends and go to church.[49]

The need for more chapels was everywhere. Whitefield

46 Whitefield, "The Indwelling of the Spirit, the Common Privilege of All Believers,"
    Selected Sermons.
47 Whitefield, "The Folly and Danger of Parting with Christ for the Pleasures and Profits of
    Life," *Selected Sermons.*
48 Whitefield, "The Indwelling of the Spirit, the Common Privilege of All Believers,"
    Selected Sermons.
49 Seymour, *Life and Times of Selina*, 1:477–78.

worked to raise up more evangelical preachers, while Lady Huntingdon labored to provide them places to worship.[50] Preaching venues sprang up across England's cities and towns. Sometimes they were chapels like the one at Bath; other times they were rented meeting halls or barns. Often Lady Huntingdon encouraged the local people to fund their own buildings, but then would add a generous contribution to help get them off the ground.[51] Within a few years, she was responsible for 116 preaching places and a seminary to train more preachers.[52]

The End of a Partnership

But this was as far as Whitefield and his patroness would travel together. She, who had outlived her husband and most of her children, now had to say goodbye to her dear friend and partner in ministry. In November of 1770 she received the following letter from Richard Cary in Boston:

> *Most Noble Lady,*
> *In God's providence an important and sorrowful event took place yesterday, in which I believe your Ladyship to be interested. I mean the death of that truly excellent and faithful servant of Christ, the Reverend Mr. Whitefield. He came from Portsmouth in New Hampshire the evening before, but was overtaken the next morning about six o'clock with an asthmatic fit.*

---

50   Dallimore, *George Whitefield*, 2:391
51   Cook, *Selina*, 343.
52   Cook, *Selina*, 406.

How happy for him to go immediately from earth to
heaven, to be at once delivered from all manner of evil
and put into possession of all possible good.

His last visit to New England has been kindly
received and his lively method of preaching the gospel
met with universal approval. Being favored with his
acquaintance, I have heard him speak in the highest
and most respectful manner of your Ladyship.

Your most dutiful and obedient servant,

Richard Cary[53]

The day before his death, although he was not feeling well, Whitefield had been persuaded to preach what became his final sermon. With the day almost gone and his health already poor, a friend cautioned him, "Sir, you are more fit to go to bed than to preach."

"True, sir," responded Whitefield. But then the preacher turned his attention heavenward and prayed, "Lord Jesus, I am weary in your work, but not of it. If I have not yet finished my course, let me go and speak for you once more in the fields and come home and die."[54]

After almost two hours of expounding on the relationship between faith and works in the plan of salvation, God enabled Whitefield to do exactly as he prayed. Whitefield had preached at least 18,000 sermons, averaging more than ten a week—more

---

53 Tyson and Schlenther, *Midst*, 111.
54 Cook, *Selina*, 280–81.

than 500 a year for thirty-four consecutive years.[55] At fifty-five years old, Whitefield knew his body had worn out. He closed his final sermon by saying, "I have outlived many on earth but they cannot outlive me in heaven. I shall soon be in a world where time, age, pain and sorrow are unknown. My body fails, my spirit expands. How willingly would I live forever to preach Christ. But I die to be with Him!"[56]

In Whitefield's will, he left everything to his patroness.[57] Lady Huntingdon carried on in her oversight of preachers and properties, saying, "To serve all gospel ministers is our highest honor and happiness."[58] Funding her seminary students' clothes, food, and ministry trips took half of her annual income, but these young men planted new churches, preached in her chapels, and took the good news of Jesus to the remote and unreached areas of England.[59]

Lady Huntingdon's continued drive to advance the gospel, led her in 1790 to want to lease a large theater that had been used for horse shows in East London and convert it into another chapel. One of her senior advisors counseled against it.

"We would need £500 to finance the new chapel," he told her, "but the funds aren't there."

While Lady Huntingdon listened to his objections, the mail arrived. Upon opening one of the letters, her eyes filled with tears. She pulled out a check for exactly £500.

---

55 E. A. Johnston, *George Whitefield: A Definitive Biography* (Tentmaker, 2009), 2:504–505.
56 Pollock, *George Whitefield*, 270.
57 Cook, *Selina*, 316.
58 Seymour, *Life and Times of Selina*, 1:114.
59 Cook, *Selina*, 309–10, 313, 332.

"Take this and pay for the chapel," she said to her advisor, "and be no longer faithless but believing."[60]

A Partnership of Revival

What Lady Huntingdon and George Whitefield accomplished was truly incalculable. They reached into the unreached places of both England and America where there were no faithful churches and no gospel preachers. Together they persuaded many of England's nobility that God was not a dull idea, but a living Savior who could be known and felt. In the years before the American colonies became an independent nation, four-fifths of Americans had heard Whitefield preach Jesus.[61]

Whitefield's broad-reaching evangelism gave America a united theological backbone that shaped the nation for generations to come. In total, Whitefield evangelized upward of ten million people and no one could begin to count the number of conversions he saw. Together, this gospel preacher and his Gospel Patron brought their generation face to face with eternity and revived the faith of the English-speaking world.[62]

---

60 Cook, *Selina*, 405–6. (Again I'm entirely indebted to Faith Cook for this marvelous scene and have adapted the language a little bit for dialogue.)
61 Johnston, *George Whitefield*, 2:504–5.
62 Johnston, *George Whitefield*, 2:504–5; see also Dallimore, *George Whitefield*, 2:412.

And who knows whether you have not come to the kingdom for such a time as this?

ESTHER 4:14

4 The Resurgence of Evangelical Churches

Newton
& Thornton

Despite Whitefield and Lady Huntingdon's massive impact on the Christianity of England, 10,000 Church of England churches remained stale and lifeless.[1] Like many times before in history, the men who were supposed to be men for God retreated from the old doctrines of Christianity, and the masses mistakenly thought of themselves as "decent Christian people."[2] Most Englishmen sat in their pews week after week but never encountered the God of the Bible.[3] Instead of real Christianity, they were fed a cheap imitation and didn't even know it.

Religion was kept in its official place, all dressed up and outwardly impressive, but the salt had lost its saltiness. The Church of England, like a tired old man, seemed ready to lay down and give up the ghost.

It was up to the next generation to spread God's movement among the church. And this work began with a former slave-trader and an uneducated merchant, both named John.

1   Jonathan Aitken, *John Newton: From Disgrace to Amazing Grace* (Wheaton, Ill.: Crossway, 2007), 285; see also John S. Simon, *The Revival of Religion in England in the Eighteenth Century* (London : C. H. Kelly, [1900?]). Simon says, "The immediate effects of Methodism upon the Church were rather to make Churchmen set their faces all the more against the religion of feeling rather than attract them to it," 276.
2   Eric Metaxas, *William Wilberforce and the Heroic Campaign to End Slavery* (New York: HarperOne, 2007), 169.
3   Metaxas, *William Wilberforce*, 45–46.

The Younger Son

It is common knowledge that children of all ages love a good story, and in a small town sixty miles north of London there lived a man with many stories to tell.

"Mr. Newton, Mr. Newton!" rang a young boy's voice.

"Little Billy!" responded a jovial man, dressed in a sailor's jacket. "Welcome back to Olney. I see you brought your Aunt Hannah along."[4]

The dignified woman asked respectfully, "May he join the other children for your meeting today?"

"Of course, Hannah."

"I see you have quite a crowd of them again," she said.

"I remember when eighty-nine felt like a lot. Now we're over two hundred each week."[5]

"Billy adores you, you know. He loves to say he has two Uncle Johns, you and my brother."

"How is your brother?" asked Newton. "It's time I wrote to him again."

"He and Lucy are well. I tease him about turning fifty," she said with a smile.

"Hannah, I can never thank your brother enough. When I first arrived in this town, the church was so poor that it could only pay me £40 a year, barely enough to get by on. But one Sunday your brother rode his horse all the way from London to hear me preach. After the sermon, he did something I never

---

4   Kevin Belmonte, *William Wilberforce: A Hero for Humanity* (Grand Rapids, Mich.: Zondervan, 2007), 26; Metaxas, *William Wilberforce*, 10.

5   Aitken, *John Newton*, 188.

expected. He said, 'Be hospitable, Newton! Keep an open house to entertain the poor and the needy. I will send you £200 a year and readily send more whenever you have need.'[6]

"Yes, that's my brother," said Hannah unsurprised. "Lucy is the same—always giving. But I suspect no one knows the truth about him quite like you do."

"Great men are often misunderstood," replied Newton.

Just then they spotted a group of boys climbing on gravestones in the church yard.

"Boys," Newton called out in a fatherly tone while rushing in their direction.

He ushered the delinquents inside the church and when Hannah caught up with them she saw children of all ages gathered for their weekly meeting. She admired Newton's love for them. Their parents were poor farmers and lace workers and Newton saw the need for a children's ministry and started one immediately upon his arrival in Olney.[7] Hannah helped a few girls find seats as Newton began his story.

"Today's story is about a father who had two sons.[8] Now how many of you boys have a brother?" he said raising his hand. "I want you to imagine how your father would feel if when he came home from work tonight your brother said, 'Dad, I can't wait for you to die so that I can have your money.' Jesus told a

6   In today's currency, £200 would have been well over $50,000, according to Kevin Belmonte, *Hero for Humanity*; see also Milton M. Klein, *"An Amazing Grace": John Thornton and the Clapham Sect*, (New Orleans: University Press of the South, 2004), 59; Aitken, *John Newton*, 190.
7   Aitken, *John Newton*, 182, 188, 224.
8   Aitken, *John Newton*, 188.

story about a younger brother who did exactly this. He said, 'Father, give me the share of property that is coming to me. I want my inheritance now.'[9]

"It was a highly offensive request, but surprisingly the father gave his son what he asked for. He divided his property between his two sons, and not many days later the younger son sold his father's property, gathered all he had, and took a journey into a far country. He went far from his home, his family, and everyone he knew. And he wasted all of his father's money on worthless things, living only for himself."

Here Newton paused and looked around. "This story is not only a Bible story, but it's also my life's story. I was much like this younger son," he said in a low voice. "When I was eighteen years old, I traveled far from home and far from my father on a ship called the Harwich. I had been forced into the Royal Navy and lived like a typical sailor, swearing and blaspheming. The other seamen made me scrub the decks, climb up the ship's ropes in high seas, and furl and unfurl the sails in high winds. At one port I tried to run away but was caught and whipped. Eventually my captain transferred me to a slave ship named Pegasus, where I only continued in my foolishness. I was miserable just like the younger son in our story."

Hannah noticed that the children were unusually quiet. She saw Billy wedged in between a couple of ragged boys, all of whom were captivated by Newton.

"After the younger son spent all his father's money a severe

9   Luke 15:11–32.

famine arose in that country. Now who knows what a severe famine is? Wait. Raise your hand, please. Okay, Maddie."

"Umm ... umm ..."

"Yes, go ahead."

"I forgot," she squeaked. The children giggled.

"I know," said another boy confidently. "It's a special kind of badger." More giggles ensued.

"Not quite," said Newton, biting his lip to fight back laughter.

"Is it when you're crying?" said a pint-size boy with floppy hair.

"Well ... it could be," said Newton now chuckling. "Yes, Sam."

"It's when people need food really, really badly."

"That's right, Sam. The younger son needed food, so he asked someone from that country to give him a job, but the only job he could find was to feed pigs. He became so hungry that even pig food started looking good to him."

"Eeew," said a few girls in unison.

"Yuck!" "Disgusting!" exclaimed two boys.

"Exactly. Pigs ate these bitter black berries, but the younger son was not given anything to eat.[10] When he had left his father he thought he was free because he had money to do whatever he wanted, but the truth is that even though he had been rich, he was still a slave to his foolishness and sin. And I was a lot like him," Newton noted.

"After I got transferred to the Pegasus, I wound up overseeing

---

10   Kenneth Bailey, *Poet and Peasant & Through Peasant Eyes: A Literary Cultural Approach to the Parables in Luke* (Grand Rapids, Mich.: Eerdmans, 1983), 173.

slaves on the Plantain Islands, off the west coast of Africa.[11] However my new master's mistress hated me, and as soon as he was out of sight she made sure I was given only a little water to drink and the left-overs from her plate to eat. I was starving. So late in the night I went out into the fields to dig up roots to eat, but the roots only made me sick. Later on, my master believed a rumor that I had stolen his property, and he put me in iron chains like the rest of the slaves. There I was, twenty-one years-old, shackled, starving, and enslaved, wasting my life in foolishness just like the younger son in our story."

Newton paused and looked at the floor. The children watched him in silence. He shook his head as if awaking from a bad dream, looked up, and said more strongly, "But the Bible tells us that at last the younger son came to himself and said, 'How many of my father's hired servants have more than enough bread, but I'm dying of hunger! I will arise and go to my father and I will say to him, "Father, I have sinned against heaven and before you. I am no longer worthy to be called your son. Treat me as one of your hired servants."

"So he got up and headed home. On the way, he kept rehearsing his speech about how to repay the money. But while he was still a long way off, his father saw him, felt compassion, and ran to him. Fathers didn't run back then. It was seen as humiliating. But this father cared more about his son, so he ran to him and then hugged him and kissed him. When the son remembered his speech, he started in on it. But the father interrupted him to

---

11   Aitken, *John Newton*, 55–57.

give orders to the servants, saying, 'Bring quickly the best robe, and put it on him, and put a ring on his hand, and shoes on his feet. And bring the fattened calf and kill it, and let us eat and celebrate. For this my son was dead, and is alive again; he was lost, and is found.' And the whole village began to celebrate with music and dancing and good food."

"When I first read this story, I was as lost as the younger son," he declared. "But I sent my father a letter, and like the father in our story, my father sent a merchant ship to find me and bring me home. You see, if we come a little way to God, he runs to meet us while we are still a long way off.[12] God ran to meet all of us by sending his son Jesus into the world. Jesus saw us in our sin and he came to save us. He said, 'I am the way, the truth, and the life. No one comes to the Father except through me.'[13] Through Jesus' death on the cross we can all come home, and God the Father will welcome us, not as servants, but as sons. Let's pray together."

Letters between Like-Minded Men

Although some of the children were hearing it for the first time that day, Newton's testimony had become famous across England, thanks to his best-selling autobiography, *An Authentic Narrative*. Although many people had found the book riveting, none had been more moved by it than the London businessman John Thornton. A prereleased copy found its way to Thornton

---

12   Charles Spurgeon, "Prodigal Love for the Prodigal Son" (March 29, 1891), http://www.spurgeon.org/sermons/2236.htm.

13   John 14:6.

and right away Thornton could tell that Newton was a man for God, unlike so many of the religious leaders of their day. Over the next few years the two Johns formed an unusual friendship, exchanging hundreds of letters.

Their letters were honest and unguarded. The men shared prayer requests and confessed sin to one another.[14] They wrote about doctrine, how to help the poor, and the condition of their nation. Reading excerpts from the letters provides a glimpse into their rich friendship.[15]

JOHN NEWTON TO JOHN THORNTON

If I look abroad round the kingdom, I see sin and infidelity in triumph and judgment at the door, yet almost every one sleeping in security. The bulk of the people are careless and unimpressed.[16]

JOHN THORNTON TO JOHN NEWTON

When my brother Conyers and I reached Glasgow we found the same general departure from religion as in England. The gentry seem all gone off and only a few of the nobility and the poor seem to think a day of account will ever come.

How strange and yet how true, few preach Jesus, even

---

14 Thornton to Newton, August 10, 1779.

15 The unpublished letters between Thornton Newton are from the collection Thornton Papers found in Cambridge University Library's Archive Room. All subsequent excerpts in this chapter come from the author's own transcription of these letters unless otherwise noted.

16 September 28, 1776

*of Gospel Ministers. London has 97 parish churches but
only two or three men who preach the gospel.*[17]

In eighteenth-century England, wealthy patrons controlled
church pulpits. Under this system of "livings" royalty, nobility and land owners could purchase the right to appoint their
favorite preachers to a particular church. Sadly, many lazy
and lukewarm clergymen filled the position, but not the calling. They were more interested in politics, hunting, or a good
income than the work of God. John Thornton had no toler-
ance for this and looked for ways to turn the tables. Over time,
Thornton purchased eleven livings and filled them with gospel-
preaching men.[18]

Newton understood his patron's role and constantly encouraged him to play his part well.

NEWTON TO THORNTON

*May the Lord grant that all the doors He honors you
as an instrument in opening for His gospel, may be as
suitably filled.*[19]

*May the Lord abundantly prosper all that He has gra-
ciously put in your heart to attempt for the support of
His cause and people.*[20]

---

17   Aug 20, 1774; *Klein, Clapham Sect*, 3; Letters: Thornton to Bull, May 13, 1786.
18   Stephen Tomkins, *The Clapham Sect: How Wilberforce's Circle Transformed Britain*
      (Oxford: Lion Hudson, 2010), 24.
19   October 19, 1775
20   May 18, 1775

*May your endeavors to bring the gospel into Clapham
not be disappointed, but benefit and comfort thousands. Surely there is nothing worth living for but to be
instrumental in promoting His service.*[21]

Ministry Holidays

Thornton surrounded himself with preachers; they were his
best friends. One of his favorite ways to spend time with them
was to take them along on all-expense paid vacations. He often
invited Newton to join him on these trips.

THORNTON TO NEWTON

Dear Newton,

*We reached Canterbury with our own horses the first
night. Our quarters here are quite rural. We have
a view of the sea and yesterday saw the whole West
India fleet pass by. Very near us we have engaged two
bedrooms for visitors and if at any time you can make it
convenient to give us your company I shall endeavor to
return you to Mrs. Newton no worse for your journey.*

*The house I have taken belongs to Dr. Pinnell. We
had a cook come from London and another maid, a
coachmen and footman. Ours is a comical family and
yet not a disorderly one. We are just getting settled and
from my window I see all the good things going. We*

---

21   June 13, 1776

had an opportunity of picking up beef, oysters, ducks,
chickens, etc. Milk, butter, straw, and hay are difficult
articles to provide, but by means of Mr. Harvey the
rector I hope to get plenty of everything. I think I will
stay a month. We shall both be glad to see you when-
ever you can make it convenient and for whatever time
you please.

    It is a great apple year. The scent of them and hops
regaled us repeatedly as we came. We have much to be
thankful for if we look round us on every side, but when
we examine ourselves there we find much work indeed.
Blessed be God for His unspeakable gift. Pray, remem-
ber us to Mrs. Newton and all inquiring friends and
believe me,

Yours affectionately,
John Thornton[22]

Fresh air, good food, and good company were the backbone of these holidays. Thornton and his traveling companions lived very well. "You can't conceive of a finer situation," he wrote to Newton, "we all seem to be strengthened by coming here."[23]

One of Thornton's most frequent companions was his dear friend, the Reverend William Bull, whom he called "Bully." Once on a trip to Ireland, the two men were walking along the

22   September 15, 1780
23   August 16, 1783.

harbor when Thornton took an interest in a few ships that had just arrived.[24]

"What have you got on board?" he inquired of a sailor.

"Who are you?" returned a rough voice.

"Just a curious Englishman," Thornton replied.

"Oh." The reply was slightly softer this time. "In that case, it's tallow."

"Any offers yet?" asked Thornton.

"We've just come in!" barked the sailor.

"Good," said Thornton. "Tell your captain if he can give me a good price, I'll buy all of it."

While the seaman hurried off, Bull questioned, "What are you going to do with all of that?"

"Soap," he said simply, as a subtle smile of victory spread across his face.

"Soap?" questioned Bull.

"I have a soap factory outside of Hull and thought this would fund our trip's expenses."

Even on vacation, Thornton would not miss an opportunity for profit, but neither would he miss an opportunity to advance the gospel. These holidays doubled as ministry trips, in which his companions preached regularly in village churches, as William Bull records in his letters.

---

24 Josiah Bull, *The Memoirs of the Rev. William Bull* (London: James Nisbet and Co., 1864), 139.

WILLIAM BULL TO HIS WIFE

*Yesterday morning I preached at seven o'clock at Mr
Wesley's place; at ten I went to church and heard Mr
Foster; at two I preached in the meeting, which was
exceedingly crowded. At night I preached in a smaller
meeting, and the place so full that I was almost killed
with the heat; but I am very well today.*

Thornton kept an energetic schedule and at times Bull had
trouble keeping up.

WILLIAM BULL TO HIS WIFE

*On this trip to Yarmouth, we rise at six, walk to the
sea at seven, return at eight, breakfast and speak till
half-past nine, write letters till eleven when the post
goes out, ride at twelve, and return to dinner at three,
smoke a pipe, and then walk outside for an hour,
return at half-past five to tea, and most evenings go out
to preach.*[25]

BULL TO NEWTON

*If much preaching and hearing are signs of usefulness,
my visit here is very useful indeed. However, I am glad
we are on the move otherwise, between Mr. Thornton*

---

25   Bull, *Memoirs*, 151–52, 153–54.

and the people, I shall preach all the flesh off my bones.
I want to go to Newport and study humility.[26]

Thornton was a big-hearted man who focused his life on promoting the gospel wherever he could. And even though Bull knew he was expected to preach, he also knew that Thornton lavishly took care of everything else: "Mr. Thornton's kindness and love keep us all in good spirits, while his generous heart and good purse procure us the best of everything the place will afford, wherever we come. His company would make a journey through the deserts of Arabia cheerful and pleasant."[27]

Young and Very Wealthy

Thornton's business endeavors began humbly. He bypassed college and went right to work in his family's business of international trade. He soon found he had a knack for trade with Russia, and by the time he was thirty had amassed a large fortune, and later became the wealthiest businessman in all of England. With the temptations attached to his increasing riches, Thornton again called upon his friend in Olney, John Newton.

THORNTON TO NEWTON

I have been indulging this morning in meditation and prayer and was glad to remain quiet till noon and devote a few hours to the remembrance of Proverbs 10:22, "The blessing of the LORD makes rich, and He adds no

---

26 Bull, *Memoirs*, 156.
27 Bull, *Memoirs*, 137.

sorrow with it," which I can put my amen to. You will, I dare say, help us with your prayers. May the Lord keep every one of us looking with a single eye to Him, that we may not disgrace our holy profession.[28]

Newton replied, writing letters every two weeks and often reminding Thornton that great wealth can be subdued under God because "the gospel can triumph over all that is in man."[29] Newton kept him grounded.

NEWTON TO THORNTON

How worthless will money be found by those who overvalue it now, in the hour of death and in the day of judgment. The hour is coming when everything else will appear trifling and vain, but not so the knowledge and service of Jesus.[30]

An Amazing Book of Hymns

Eventually, more than 500 of Newton's letters were published during his lifetime, many of which included hymns he had written.[31] Thornton loved receiving these hymns and encouraged Newton to publish a hymnbook. Little did they know that one of the Olney Hymns would become a global anthem.[32]

---

28   February 10, 1774

29   March 4, 1775; see also February 11, 1778 & April 17, 1775.

30   March 17, 1779

31   Aitken, *John Newton*, 244.

32   Aitken, *John Newton*, 237.

THORNTON TO NEWTON

*I think you are right in printing your hymns. I shall
be glad of a thousand of them in a cheap covers
to disperse.*[33]

NEWTON TO THORNTON

*I have been enabled at length to finish the task of pre-
paring my hymns for the press. I have called it mine,
but I consider it as yours. Though I have not the vanity
to dedicate any of my services to you in public, yet
pleasure as well as gratitude prompt me to think of you
in private, under the Lord to whose goodness I owe your
friendship, as my patron. I should be loathed to take
any step of importance without your judgment. Your
approval is the greatest satisfaction and reward I can
wish to receive from a fellow creature.*

*As you have been pleased to offer to take a thousand
copies upon your own account, I entirely submit the
choice of the printer or bookseller. If they were printed
on my account and any profit should accrue to me from
the sale, I should only wish to throw it in the current
stock for supplying expenses and thereby lessening
so far for a time, the burden which you are pleased to
bear in my concerns. For I believe my mind would not
be quite easy, if I was to hoard up anything that might
arise from the sale of spiritual things. Where the Lord*

---

33   December 3, 1778.

may enable me to write, I would write for Him and look for no abiding advantage, but in the hope of His favoring my attempts for His service with His unction and blessing.

But as I said before, I have only written just as I might speak if I had the pleasure of seeing you. I shall not think the affair is managed rightly, except you are pleased to determine every part of it.

Mrs. Newton has been tolerably well for near a fortnight. We join in our best respects to you and to Mrs. Thornton. I am, Dearest Sir,

Your most obedient and obliged servant,

John Newton

February 13, 1779

By June of 1779, the hymns were printed, and Thornton's investment in the first 1,000 copies propelled it to become a best seller. This caught the attention of book store owners, who promptly stocked it. Within a year, the hymnbook went through five editions and showed no signs of stopping.[34]

Tucked away in the first section as Number 41 was a hymn called "Faith's Review and Expectation." This simple hymn used mostly one syllable words to powerfully weave together biblical theology and Newton's own testimony.[35] Initially, it did not attract a lot of attention, but as the song crossed the Atlantic, it caught on with Christians of every denomination in

34 Aitken, *John Newton*, 246, 231.
35 Aitken, *John Newton*, 226, 228.

the United States and became "the most sung, most recorded, and most loved hymn in the world."[36] The Americans knew the song as "Amazing Grace."

Waking Up the City

Three months after the Olney Hymns launched, a new opportunity arose that would soon open many new doors for the gospel.

Near the Bank of England and the Royal Exchange was a church named St. Mary Woolnoth. London's movers and shakers passed within walking distance of this church every day. John Thornton also had his office nearby. In the fall of 1779, St. Mary Woolnoth's pastor died unexpectedly, opening the door for a new man to lead this strategic church.

Thornton owned a share in the living and immediately invited Newton to join him in London. Thornton knew that if a gospel-preaching man were in the center of the city, opportunities for evangelism were sure to abound. Under Newton's leadership and Thornton's patronage, the country church in Olney had grown from 200 to 600 people and regularly attracted many visitors. Week after week for sixteen years, Newton had taught his people the doctrines of the Bible, but now the time had come to move on.[37] He penned a reply to Thornton.

NEWTON TO THORNTON

I thankfully accept your most obliging offer. I trust it is not your appointment only, but the Lord's. What un-

---

36   Aitken, *John Newton*, 224, 237.
37   Newton to Thornton, July 15, 1775.

known events and consequences depend upon the step
I am about to take! But though unknown to me, they
are known and present to Him. His servant I am and
next to Him and in subordination to Him, I am under
the strongest ties, both of affection and obligation, to
you that one creature can be to another. If He calls me
to London, He can fit me for so different a scene and
support me in it.

Your most obedient and obliged servant,
John Newton
September 20, 1779

Within weeks of Newton's arrival in London, the pews of St. Mary Woolnoth filled up. The crowds who sang his hymns and read his books came to hear him preach.

"Excuse me, but this is my pew," announced a middle-aged woman with polite annoyance.

"Please, sit down everyone," rang an official-sounding voice from the front.

"I'd like to," replied the woman under her breath, "but my seat is taken again."

"Yours, mine, and everyone's," said an elderly man brushing past her. "I liked the old days."

"This place feels as full as an egg. At least that's how Newton describes it," she said.[38] "But he doesn't seem to mind. Said something about that's why he came to London and all that."

---

38   Aitken, *John Newton*, 273.

Huddled in the back of the church, the standing-room-only-crowd swelled like a balloon being filled with air. Voices clamored.

"Shh, he's about to begin," hushed a woman tiptoeing to see over the people standing in front of her.

Newton began with a passage of Scripture: "Jeremiah chapter five, verse twenty-nine, 'Shall I not visit for these things, declares the LORD, and shall not my soul be avenged on such a nation as this?' Three times the Lord God repeats, by his prophet, this alarming question. The Lord, the Governor of the earth, has provided in the history of one nation, a lesson of instruction and warning to every nation under the sun."

The preacher warned his audience, "Like Israel, we are a highly favored people, and have long enjoyed privileges which excite the admiration and envy of surrounding nations; and we are also a sinful, ungrateful people. When we compare the blessings and mercies we have received from the Lord with our conduct towards Him, it is to be feared we are no less concerned with the question in my text than Israel was of old. This is the point I purpose to illustrate.

"We have enjoyed such an uninterrupted series of peace and prosperity as cannot be paralleled in the history of any nation we have heard of," Newton said. "But if I could make a tour of the kingdom with a stranger and show him what is transacting in the busy and in the cheery world, in city, court, and country; if I could describe to him the persons he would see at our theatres and public places, at the race track, at contested elections, and explain the motives and aims which bring them together; if

I could introduce him into the families of the great, the reputed wise, and the wealthy, along with the ignorance and licentiousness of the populace, he could not but perceive that infidelity, pride, sensuality, greediness of gain, strangely coupled with contempt of God, and a daring opposition to His will, constitute the leading features of our portrait as a nation."[39]

Newton continued, "In a word, the Gospel of Christ, the truth as it is in Jesus, is little known amongst us and where it is published it is rejected by a great majority of every rank. We have just reason to expect the Lord should speak to us in His displeasure and avenge Himself of such a nation as this.[40]

"What hope do we have?" he cried out. "Oh! that I could prevail on you to earnestly seek the LORD, while He may be found. You cannot serve or love or trust Him unless you be born again and till this is done, you are neither fit to live, nor fit to die. But Jesus is exalted to produce this change in the heart of a sinner, by the power of His Holy Spirit and to give faith, repentance, and remission of sins. Jesus said, 'Whoever comes to me, I will never cast out.' May we turn to the Lord from whom we have so greatly revolted.[41] O Lord, convince them by your own power! Open the blind eyes, unstop the deaf ears, and turn the stony hearts into flesh. Amen."

---

39 Works of John Newton, *The Guilt and Danger of Such a Nation as This*, (New York: Williams & Whiting, 1810) 142–43.
40 Newton, *Guilt and Danger*, 153, 159.
41 Newton, *Guilt and Danger*, 164–65.

Newton's words rang out with power. From his new post in London, all kinds of people now had access to his teaching, and he reflected on these expanding opportunities in a letter to another minister.

NEWTON TO REV. JOSHUA SYMONDS

Dear Sir,

If the Lord had left me to choose my situation, London would have been almost the last place I should have chosen. But now that I am fixed here I seem to prefer it. My sphere of service is extremely enlarged and my sphere of usefulness likewise. My hearers are made up of all sorts. Churchmen and Dissenters, Calvinists and Arminians, Moravians and Methodists, now and then I believe Papists and Quakers sit quietly to hear me. If he loves Jesus, I will love him; whatever name he may be called by.[42]

Newton preached for three weekly church services, but now that he was in the city, well-connected urbanites would host dinner parties for their business partners and influential friends and invite Newton to come and preach to them.[43] In these "house preaching" assignments, men like Thornton set the table, while Newton set forth the gospel. Through Thornton and Newton's joint influence, the gospel was advancing all

---

42   John Newton to the Rev. Joshua Symonds, Letter V, March 29, 1781.

43   Aitken, *John Newton*, 276.

over London, most notably among one young Member of Parliament who sought a secret meeting with Mr. Newton.

Wilber

In early December of 1785, about six years after he began preaching in London, Newton sat at home in No. 13 Charles Square eagerly awaiting his clandestine guest. What he didn't know was that the visitor's own nervousness had caused him to take two laps around the tree-lined square before finally approaching Newton's door. At last there was a knock. The aging preacher answered the door and swept his guest inside.

"Come in, come in," invited Newton, leading his guest to the parlor and pouring him a cup of tea.

"I didn't know whom else to turn to, sir, but I remembered my visits to Olney with Aunt Hannah and Uncle William. I remembered your stories about life at sea and how God saved you."

"I once was blind, but now I see," said the preacher smiling. "Only, shall I still call you Little Billy? Perhaps William is better suited for a Member of Parliament, or even Master Wilberforce?"

"My friends call me Wilber."

"All right, Wilber it is," said Newton with an air of finality. "It's been, what, fifteen years? You were like a son to me and I've never ceased to pray for you and have often hoped God would bring you to me."[44]

"Well, I'm grateful you're in London now," said the young man.

---

44 Personal Communication with Marylynn Rouse who shared with me an unpublished symposium paper "A Double Portion of My Thoughts and Prayers" (2002), p. 4.

"You can thank your Uncle John Thornton for that," said Newton cheerfully.

"Uncle John … I can still remember when I was a boy, I must have been about twelve, when he gave me a large sum of money, much more than a normal gift for a young boy because he wanted to teach me to give to the poor."[45]

"That's Thornton," said Newton. "For him giving is like breathing, if he stops he'll die."

Wilberforce laughed. "Yes, I've heard he devotes large sums to promote the cause of religion and assist many clergymen."[46]

Newton smiled but said nothing. Over the next several hours he heard the unexpected news firsthand that despite all the people and pressures that tried to drag William Wilberforce away from the truth he learned as a boy, the prodigal son was returning home.

"Wilber!" Newton exclaimed enthusiastically, "Praise the Lord for your growing convictions."

"Indeed," said Wilberforce. "But now I'm confused about what to do. Should I stay in Parliament or leave politics for church work?"[47]

"That is a question for God to answer," said Newton, "but you'll not forget the example of your uncle. For many years now I have seen Thornton serve Jesus in business as much as any man in the church, maybe more."

"But how?" Wilberforce asked. "Already I feel that there

---

45 Belmonte, *Hero for Humanity*, 28.
46 Personal Communication with Kevin Belmonte and he shared with me his unpublished paper "Channels of Beneficence" (2005), 12; Klein, *Clapham Sect*, 125.
47 Metaxas, *William Wilberforce*, 49.

would be so many temptations and great opposition to an evangelical Christian in the House."

For a moment, Newton looked up toward the ceiling. It was as if he were solving a puzzle in the depths of his own mind. "I know," he burst out and began shuffling through some papers on his desk. If you'll give me a minute, I may be able to help you."

Wilberforce took a few sips of tea as Newton bustled about. Eventually, he uncovered the buried treasure.

"Wilber, I want you to hear how this can be done in your Uncle's own words. I'm sure he wouldn't mind if I read to you from a few of his letters. Here's one, listen to this."

THORNTON TO NEWTON

> There is always a multiplicity of business that must be attended to and often my natural hastiness of spirit ensnares me. I have been studying doctrines with some effort for many years and my present lesson is to practice Psalm 46:10, "Be still and know that I am God." I hope to see where my strength is and not to go forth foolishly as in times past, but to take heed that one like the Son of God is on my right hand.[48]

"And here's another. Oh, this one is really good," Newton said excitedly.

---

48   June 1, 1775

THORNTON TO NEWTON

Jesus reigns and He will preserve His justified ones.
May the Lord strengthen us that we may grow in grace
and in the knowledge of Him and our hearts leap with-
in us every time we hear His sweet name articulated.
May the Lord keep us earnest for the salvation of our
dear friends and relatives and all around us. Let us not
with Peter be disturbed with the high winds and storms
of life, but keeping our eye riveted on Jesus go through
good report and evil report steadfast, unmovable, ever
abounding in the work of the Lord as knowing He will
perform what He has spoken to us of.[49]

"Keeping our eye riveted on Jesus," said Newton. "What a line! And this focus on Jesus united with an earnestness, like he said, 'for the salvation of all around us' is how your uncle has served the Lord as a businessman. These two things are his primary business. He has found that you don't need a position or a paycheck to fix your eyes on Jesus and play a part in his work of saving lost people. Wilber, don't rule out Parliament just yet. I can imagine that the Lord would make you useful in public life and cause you to be a blessing, both as a Christian and a statesman. And why don't you go round and catch up with your uncle again soon?"

---

49   July 7, 1774

Finding God's Path

Wilberforce took Newton's advice and two days later dined with the Thorntons and his aunt Hannah Wilberforce. Afterward he wrote in his journal:

> *Dec. 9th*
> *Dined at Mrs. Wilberforce's—Mr. Thornton there. How unaffectedly happy he is—oh that I were like him.*

Wilberforce was twenty-six years old, eloquent, charismatic, and popular. Yet the cheerfulness of Newton and Thornton attracted him like a magnet. In them he saw that Christians were not gloomy, but joyful. Less than a month after their dinner, Wilberforce received a letter of encouragement from Thornton.

THORNTON TO WILBERFORCE

> *My dear Sir,*
> *You may easier conceive than I can express the satisfaction I had from a few minutes conversation with Mr. Newton yesterday afternoon.*
> *I am aware of your difficulties which are many and call for great prudence and caution. Those that believe must not make haste, but be content to go God's pace and watch the leadings of His providence as the pillar and the cloud formerly.*
> *There is a danger in running from church to church to hear. More profit is obtained under one or two settled ministers.*

I shall at any time be glad to see you here and I can
quarter you and let you be as retired as you please and I
hope we shall never be on a footing of ceremony. I am,
My Dear Sir,   *Your much devoted kinsman,*
John Thornton
December 24, 1785

Wilberforce immediately began attending church at St. Mary Woolnoth and kept up his visits to the Thorntons, recording one such visit in his journal:

January 3rd
By Newton's advice, went to Mr. Thornton's, dined with
them—J. Thornton perfectly happy and composed. I
will go there as often as I dare anywhere.

Letters and conversations between Newton and Wilberforce continued, and God gave the young politician the clarity he had been searching for. Wilberforce knew God's calling on his life and wrote it down in his journal:

October 28, 1787
God Almighty has set before me two great objects: the
suppression of the Slave Trade and the Reformation
of Manners [which meant morals].

For Thornton, Newton, and Wilberforce, the gospel was fundamental. Thornton loved to accelerate the ministries of men who preached the gospel. Newton played the part of a patriarch to England's future church leaders, missionaries, and leading laymen. Wilberforce wrote a best-selling book on Christian doctrine that he called "my manifesto." These men believed the foundation of justice, the engine of activism, and the catalyst of change is not politics nor morality, not votes nor campaigns, but a return to faith in Jesus Christ.[50] More than anything else, these three men were gospel men.

The Church Revived

The foresight of John Thornton to open a door for Newton in London shaped the political and spiritual future of a nation. Although Newton is most often remembered for writing "Amazing Grace" and for mentoring Wilberforce throughout his twenty-year campaign to abolish slavery in England, his fatherly wisdom and spiritual counsel also benefited Charles Simeon, William Carey, Richard Johnson, Claudius Buchanan, Hannah More, and the Clapham Circle. His enduring influence helped spread the gospel around the world.

Likewise, the Church of England, which had long been barren of gospel fruit, now had exploded with buds and blossoms on many branches. The number of gospel-preaching men had risen to more than 400 within the established church, and by the end of the next generation, evangelicals held one quarter of all Church of England pulpits.[51] Amazing grace had come and revived the church.

---

50   Metaxas, *William Wilberforce*, 167.
51   Aitken, *John Newton*, 24; Thornton to Bull, March 3, 1783; Klein, *Clapham Sect*, 137.

History remembers the names Newton and Wilberforce, but the one unknown to most of us is Thornton. This is strange in one sense because he was so well-known in his own day. When he died, the media hailed his passing, claiming that Thornton's "charities transcended belief and reached to the remotest parts of the globe."[52] Four pastors, including Newton and Bull, preached sermons in his honor; William Cowper wrote a poem in his memory; Thomas Scott penned a sixty-page discourse praising Thornton, saying that "doing good was the great business of his life." It was said of John Thornton that he was, "one of those rare men, in whom the desire to relieve distress assumes the form of a master passion."[53] Thornton lived to alleviate suffering and spread the gospel wherever he could and his friend Henry Venn said it best:

> *Few followers of the Lamb have ever done more to feed the hungry, clothe the naked, and help all that suffer adversity; and to spread the savor of the knowledge of Christ crucified. Were there but one thousand loving Christians of great opulence in Britain, like-minded with John Thornton ... the nation would be judged and convinced of the good operation of the gospel.*[54]

In his final hours, Thornton called for his sons Samuel, Robert, and Henry to stand by his side. He told them, "My

---

52 Klein, *Clapham Sect*, 126.
53 Klein, *Clapham Sect*, 127.
54 Klein, *Clapham Sect*, 126–27.

sons ... keep your faith in the God and Savior with whom I have walked."[55]

"Are you happy now father?" they asked.[56]

"Yes," he said. "Happy in Jesus. All things are as well as they can be. Precious, precious ...".

His strength failed before he could add the final word, but everyone listening knew what it was. To his dying breath, the focus of John Thornton's life and patronage had been Jesus.

55   Belmonte, *Channels of Beneficence*, 11.
56   Klein, *Clapham Sect*, 121.

Indeed, I count everything as loss because of the
surpassing worth of knowing Christ Jesus my Lord.
For his sake I have suffered the loss of all things
and count them as rubbish, in order
that I may gain Christ

PHILIPPIANS 3:8

5 The Gospel of Gospel Patronage

The past three chapters of this book have sought to answer the question: How has God worked through people to change the world? During my historical research of these well-known heroes of the faith and their lesser-known patrons, I've often exclaimed, "They just don't make people like that anymore."

I remember saying this to a woman named Marylynn Rouse, one of the world's leading experts on John Newton. My research had taken me to England and the quaint little town of Stratford-upon-Avon. Sitting in Marylynn's living room, amidst stacks of old books and piles of papers, I asked, "Marylynn, what made Newton, Thornton, and Wilberforce such incredible men? It just seems like they don't make men like that anymore."

"Focus," she responded simply. "They took the word of God really seriously and were whole-hearted in their commitment."

Without warning tears filled my eyes. These stories had become so real to me, and I longed to be like the main characters. But how? How do we become the kind of people God uses to change the world?

I remember being confronted with this same question as a twenty-year-old college student. School had just let out for the summer, and I found myself sitting on a big, grassy lawn in Memphis, Tennessee, surrounded by thousands of other college students. A small, balding man in his 50s walked across a massive stage and stood before the microphone. I had never heard this man speak before. I had never read his books. But his unbridled passion arrested my attention. He said:

> People who make a difference in the world are not people who have mastered a lot of things. They are people who have been mastered by a very few things that are very, very great. If you want your life to count, you don't have to have high I.Q. and you don't have to have a high E.Q.; you don't have to be smart; you don't have to have good looks; you don't have to be from a good family or from a good school. You just have to know a few basic, simple, glorious, majestic, obvious, unchanging, eternal things and be gripped by them and be willing to lay down your life for them. Which is why anybody in this crowd can make a worldwide difference, because it isn't you; it's what your gripped with."[1]

So what things must we be gripped with if we're going to make a lasting difference in our world? What things gripped Humphrey Monmouth, Lady Huntingdon, and John Thornton?

---

1   John Piper, "Boasting Only in the Cross" (May 20, 2000), http://www.desiringgod.org/resource-library/conference-messages/boasting-only-in-the-cross; or https://www.youtube.com/watch?v=7q8ptO84a58.

The Passion of the Patrons

Monmouth lived 500 years ago and sadly we don't have any of his journals, letters, or papers that would reveal his motivation in his own words. But what we can go on is his example. He knew that his partnership with Tyndale was a dangerous mission. An English New Testament was against the law and Monmouth ended up in prison for his part in creating one. Tyndale ended up dead. Humphrey Monmouth willingly moved toward risk and toward suffering for the sake of bringing his countrymen a Bible they could read and a God they could know. That is no small commitment.

Lady Huntingdon's motivation is more easily discerned—first from her own words, and second, from what others said about her. At the turning point in her life, we have three lines from her letters to her friend Phillip Doddridge that plainly spell out what she was gripped with.

On February 23, 1747, she wrote, "O! how do I lament the weakness of my hands, the feebleness of my knees, and coolness of my heart. I want it on fire always, not for self-delight, but to spread the gospel from pole to pole."

Less than a month later, a letter dated March 15, 1747, displays the depth of her emotion: "My heart wants nothing so much as to dispense all—all for the glory of Him whom my soul loves."[2]

---

2   Seymour, *Life and Times of Selina*, 1:79. (I have updated loveth to loves.)

Later that same year, on November 8, 1747, Lady Huntingdon wrote:

> *The one thing worth living for must be the proclaiming of the love of God to man in Jesus Christ. I am nothing—Christ is all. To behold the glory of such a Savior ought to make us breathe His praises from pole to pole. To preach Christ and His blessing upon repentance over the earth is the commission. May the Lord give us all such love, to live and to die to Him alone.*[3]

Others who knew her confirmed that Lady Huntingdon's life proved how real these statements were to her. George Whitefield said, "Good Lady Huntingdon is indeed a mother in Israel. She is all in a flame for Jesus."[4] The Reverend Henry Venn wrote of her, "I am favored with the pleasing sight and with the animating example of a soul inflamed with love to a crucified God."[5]

One of Lady Huntingdon's seminary students, William Aldridge, said, "She was most refreshed if some sinner had been cut down under the word and sent away weeping and seeking redemption in the blood of Jesus. I believe the news of £10,000 a year having been left her would not have been so pleasing to her as to have heard of the conversion of one soul to God."[6]

---

3   Tyson and Schlenther, *Midst*, 181–82; Seymour, *Life and Times of Selina*, 1:81–82.
4   Cook, *Selina*, 115.
5   Cook, *Selina*, 269.
6   Cook, *Selina*, 337.

Her medical doctor, who was with her in her final hours, wrote, "Her whole life seemed devoted to one great object, the glory of God and the salvation of His creatures."[7] Indeed, this was what gripped her.

John Thornton ran on this same gospel fuel. He lived to serve Jesus. Thornton once wrote in his journal: "Lord, strengthen then thy feeble servant and enable me to employ the present time as a faithful steward in thy service, looking unto thee O blessed Jesus for what I must do."[8]

His correspondence with Newton is ripe with gospel motivation, as can be seen in this excerpt from a letter dated January 6, 1774:

THORNTON TO NEWTON

Sin cannot be mortified, but by looking to Him that hung upon the cross for its atonement. And beholding the glory of God in the face, person and understanding of Jesus is the only thing that transforms and changes the soul into the same image.

Likewise, Thornton gladly supported the man who wrote the following lines:

NEWTON TO THORNTON

I see Jesus to be all desirable and all sufficient. Other foundation of my hope, other source of life, other object

7   Cook, *Selina*, 419.
8   Sunday, October 2, 1768.

of rest and happiness I neither know nor desire. I
choose Him as my portion and His will and glory are
the great scope to which I would direct all my thoughts
and aims.[9]

At another time, March 2, 1775, Newton wrote, "To live in and by and to and for and with Jesus by faith, this is life indeed."[10]

At Thornton's death, his friend Thomas Scott summed up his life in a eulogy entitled, *The Love of Christ, the Source of Genuine Philanthropy*, in which he said of Thornton, "In dispensing his bounty, it is well known, that he always aimed to promote the knowledge and practice of the religion of the Bible amongst mankind, and to bring the careless, the ignorant, the profane, the profligate, to attend to the concerns of their souls, to repent, and turn to God."

Scott described Thornton's motivation for buying up livings for ministers, saying it was, "for the sake of planting useful ministers of the gospel in those parts, where he supposed the people to be perishing for lack of knowledge." William Bull described his friend Thornton this way: "I never knew a person that lived so near to God."[11]

More proofs could be brought forth, but the jury is already unanimous. Jesus, His love, His life, His word, His death, these are the things that compelled the Gospel Patrons of history to live and give as generously and sacrificially as they did. They

---

9   August 20, 1774.
10   March 2, 1775.
11   Klein, *Clapham Sect*, 124.

saw Jesus for who He really is and were gripped with Him. He was their supreme passion, their main business, their chief concern.

More than Autopilot

So what are you gripped with? The truth is our hearts are always in flux. One day we're fired up for the right things, and the next we're distracted with secondary causes, other passions, lesser things. Work gets all-consuming. It's a busy season at home. We get run down and weary. And we coast in our pursuit of Jesus. We think, "I know Jesus, or at least I know all I need to know to cover my bases." But just as fires need continual fuel to keep burning, so do our passions. Without it, we cool.

Another challenge we face is that the world is not pro-Jesus. It's never in vogue to have a passion for Christ. It seems that everyone has a dream or a cause they care about, but following Jesus is rarely it. And we want to fit in. We want to be comfortable. So we settle for a cause everyone will applaud.

But if these first two pressures weren't enough, we also have an enemy who wants to blind us to the truth of who Jesus is. The apostle Paul warned the Corinthians of this, saying, "I am afraid that as the serpent deceived Eve by his cunning, your thoughts will be led astray from a sincere and pure devotion to Christ."[12] Our enemy knows that, "It is a fact of history that every Christian revival during the past nineteen hundred years has come, at least in part, from a fresh study of the life

---

12   2 Corinthians 11:3.

and teaching of the Christ."[13] Consequently, "one of Satan's key strategies," says New Testament scholar Clint Arnold, "is corrupting and distorting an understanding of who Jesus really is, what He came to do, and what He is about to do."[14]

Our flesh, the world, and the Devil war against a life aimed at eternity. Therefore, we cannot be on autopilot and expect to become the kind of people God uses to change the world. Instead, we need to refuel our fire, refocus our passions, and remind ourselves of Jesus. That is what the rest of this chapter is about.

No One Speaks like This Man

For the last three years of Jesus' life, crowds surrounded Him wherever He went. People would walk for days just to hear Jesus preach and the Bible tells us they "heard Him gladly."[15] They said things like:

> › *Where does this man get this wisdom?*[16]
> › *What is this? A new teaching with authority?*[17]
> › *No one has ever spoke like this man.*[18]

13   Dorothy Sayers, *The Man Born to Be King* (London: Victor Gollancz, 1943), 12.
14   Clinton E. Arnold, *3 Crucial Questions about Spiritual Warfare* (Grand Rapids, Mich.: Baker, 1997), 53.
15   Mark 8:3, 12:37.
16   Matthew 13:54; Mark 6:2.
17   Mark 1:27; Matthew 7:29.
18   John 7:46.

But Jesus' audience was also compelled to make up their minds about Him. They speculated about His identity, always asking, "Who is He?"[19]

If we are to answer that same question, the place to begin is with Jesus' own claims. Who did Jesus say He was? Below, are ten claims Jesus made concerning Himself.

1. Jesus said that He was sinless. Amidst a public debate, Jesus challenged the Jewish leaders by claiming to be innocent of sin. He said,

Which one of you convicts me of sin?[20]

This is a wild claim for anyone to make because there is no end to the evidences of our selfishness, pride, impatience, and focusing our lives on something or someone other than God; thus the familiar phrase, "Nobody's perfect." Even other religious leaders like Muhammad, Gandhi, and Mother Teresa have all admitted that they are sinners.[21] But not Jesus. Jesus said that He was sinless.

---

19 Matthew 16:13–14, 21:10.

20 John 8:46.

21 Mark Driscoll and Gerry Breshears, *Vintage Jesus: Timeless Answers to Timely Questions* (Wheaton, Ill.: Good News Publishers), 24.

2. Jesus said His words would outlast heaven and earth. Speaking to His disciples, He said,

Heaven and earth will pass away, but my words will not pass away.[22]

Most of us will be forgotten within a few generations, but Jesus said His words would extend into eternity. Who could claim such a thing?

3. Jesus said He came from heaven. He repeatedly claimed, *I have come down from heaven.*[23] Jesus emphasized the point that He was not from earth, but rather was sent to earth on a rescue mission from God the Father.

4. Jesus said He was the Messiah. A Samaritan woman said to Jesus, "I know that the Messiah is coming," and Jesus responded to her, saying,

I who speak to you am He.[24]

This claim would have been outrageous if Jesus was only a good religious teacher. The Jews had a long history of expectation for their coming Savior, and Jesus said He was it.

---

22   Matthew 24:35; Mark 13:31; Luke 21:33.
23   John 3:13; 6:33, 38, 58, 62; 7:29.
24   John 4:25–26.

5. Jesus said He was the Son of God. In an argument with the Jews, who thought He was blaspheming, Jesus answered them, *Because I said, "I am the Son of God."*[25]

The Jews of His day understood Jesus perfectly. The Bible says, "This was why the Jews were seeking all the more to kill Him, because not only was He breaking the Sabbath, but He was even calling God His own Father, making Himself equal with God."[26]

6. Jesus said He was the King of heaven.[27] He said to Pontus Pilate, *My kingdom is not of this world.*[28]

No priest, pastor, or rabbi would be taken seriously if they claimed to be the King of heaven, and yet that is exactly what Jesus claimed.

7. Jesus said that He is the only way to heaven. He said, *I am the way, and the truth, and the life. No one comes to the Father except through me.*[29]

As unpopular and offensive as this claim was and still is, Jesus did not shrink from clearly making the statement. His claim was not that He knew the way to heaven, but instead that He was the only way to heaven. At another time, He used

---

25   John 10:36.
26   John 5:18.
27   Matthew 7:21, 24:30, 26:64.
28   John 18:36–37.
29   John 14:6.

a different metaphor to say the same thing, "I am the door. If anyone enters by me, he will be saved."[30]

8. Jesus said He came to save the world. Amidst a crowd in Jerusalem, Jesus cried out,

I did not come to judge the world but to save the world.[31]

Many of us want to change the world, but Jesus claimed He came to save the world.

9. Jesus said He could forgive sin. When a paralyzed man was carried to Jesus, Jesus saw his faith and said to him,

Son, your sins are forgiven.[32]

The Jews in Jesus' day knew full well that this was a claim to deity. They said, "Who can forgive sins but God alone?"

10. Jesus said He was God. The high priest questioned Jesus' identity, saying, "Are you the Christ?"[33] Jesus answered him by quoting a verse from the Old Testament,

I am, and you will see the Son of Man seated at the right hand of Power, and coming with the clouds of heaven.[34]

Here, Jesus applied the role of God to Himself—the one seated on the throne of heaven, ruling His eternal kingdom in glory. In another incident, Jesus applied the name of God to Himself.

---

30   John 10:9.
31   John 12:47, 3:17.
32   Mark 2:5–7.
33   Mark 14:61.
34   Mark 14:62; see also Daniel 7:13–14.

In Exodus 3:15–16 God told Moses to refer to Him as "I AM," and added, "This is my name forever." When Jesus was questioned by the religious leaders, He answered them, "Truly, truly, I say to you, before Abraham was I AM."[35]

Jesus said he was God by claiming the role of God and the name of God for Himself. This is why the Jews wanted to kill Jesus. They said, "We are stoning you ... because you, a mere man, claim to be God."[36] Jesus did not say He was "like God", or the God of this world, or even one of many gods. Jesus of Nazareth, the carpenter, the son of Mary, unapologetically claimed to be God.

Preaching, Teaching, and Healing

No one else in history has ever made such enormous claims. In light of such unparalleled claims, the next question we must ask is: Was Jesus telling the truth? Anyone can talk, but did Jesus's life back up His claims?

The Bible begins Jesus' story by telling of His miraculous birth. But then, we quickly learn that Jesus had an ordinary life. His mother Mary and adoptive father Joseph went on to have at least six other kids: four boys and at least two girls.[37] Jesus was an older brother in a big family. He grew up in a small town, never traveled very far from His home, and vacationed with His family to the same spot every year.[38] We also read

35   John 8:58.
36   John 10:33 (NIV).
37   Matthew 13:55–56; Mark 6:3.
38   Luke 2:41.

that Jesus got hungry[39] and thirsty[40] and tired.[41] He ate and drank[42] and slept.[43] He had friends,[44] went to dinner parties,[45] celebrated holidays,[46] attended weddings,[47] loved children,[48] and had a job as a carpenter.[49] His three best friends were fishermen—not priests. Sinners and tax collectors and common people loved being around Him.[50] Just like us, Jesus went to church on the weekends,[51] prayed,[52] read His Bible,[53] and memorized Scripture.[54]

Additionally, Jesus was a real man with a personality and emotions just like we have. He felt joy and happiness.[55] When God was dishonored, Jesus got angry.[56] At times He even wept.[57] Jesus felt compassion toward hurting people, sick people, and hungry people and often gave to meet their needs.[58] Like many of us, Jesus experienced rejection from a best friend

---

39   Luke 4:2; Matthew 4:2; Mark 11:12.
40   John 4:7, 19:18.
41   Matthew 8:24; Mark 4:38; Luke 8:23–24.
42   Luke 7:34; Matthew 11:19.
43   Matthew 8:24; Mark 4:38; Luke 8:23–24.
44   John 11:5.
45   Luke 7:36, 11:37, 14:1, 15:2, 19:5.
46   Luke 2:41.
47   John 2:1–2.
48   Luke 18:15–17; Mark 10:13–14; Matthew 19:13–15; 21:15–16.
49   Mark 6:3.
50   Mark 2:15; Matthew 11:19; Luke 15:1.
51   Luke 4:16.
52   Luke 5:16, 6:12, 9:18, 10:21, 11:1, 22:41, 22:44.
53   Luke 4:16–19; Matthew 21:16, 42; Mark 2:25.
54   Luke 4:4, 8, 12, 16, 25–27; 6:3, 23, 26; 7:27; 11:30–32, 51; 17:26, 28–29; 20:37.
55   Luke 10:21; John 15:11, 17:13; Hebrews 12:2.
56   John 2:15; Mark 11:15; Matthew 21:12.
57   John 11:35.
58   Matthew 9:36, 14:14, 15:32; Luke 7:13.

and betrayal by another.[59] Jesus felt pain, grief, and sorrow.[60] His family often misunderstood Him.[61] He even experienced temptation to sin like we do.[62] The difference is He never gave in.[63]

Nowhere in the life of Jesus do we see that He sinned.

Not one lie.

Not one selfish motive.

Not one lustful look at a woman.

Not one ounce of greed in His heart.

Not one disrespectful word to His parents.

Not one time did He play to the crowd, seeking the praise and glory of men.[64]

Not once did He say to God the Father, "Leave me alone. I just want to do what I want to do."[65]

Instead, Jesus Christ was perfectly righteous. He wasn't swayed by people. He always obeyed God the Father.[66] It was His Father first, people second.[67] This meant Jesus kept the Ten Commandments and fulfilled every law of God.[68] He did what God the Father sent Him to do and said what God the Father led Him to say even when it was unpopular. Jesus spoke

---

59   John 18:17, 25–27, 13:21; Isaiah 53:3.
60   Matthew 23:37; Luke 19:41; Isaiah 53:3.
61   Mark 3:21, 31, 32.
62   Luke 4:2.
63   Luke 4:1–13; 1 Peter 2:22; Hebrews 2:18, 4:15; 1 John 1:5.
64   John 5:41, 12:43.
65   John 5:19.
66   John 5:30, 6:38, 8:28; Luke 22:42.
67   Matthew 6:33, 26:39; Luke 22:42.
68   Matthew 5:17.

the truth, even when it was hard for other people to hear and made life more difficult for Himself.[69]

But why does this matter? It matters because you and I are not like this. We're not holy, righteous, and good. We don't live lives set apart for God, but instead we're lovers of money, lovers of pleasure, and lovers of self. And what the Bible tells us is that 2,000 years ago there was a man just like us, who was not like us. He was human and divine. He said things that should shock and offend us. He said things that got Him killed. But strangely, there was nothing in His life to controvert His claims, no evidence to convict Him of perjury.

Instead, His life's work was preaching, teaching, and healing people. One time the mother-in-law of His friend Peter had a fever, and Jesus healed her by simply taking her hand and helping her sit up.[70] Jesus said to a paralyzed man, "Rise, pick up your mat and go home," and the paralyzed man got up and walked out.[71] A woman who had an incurable blood disease spent twelve years and all of her money going to doctors trying to get well, but when she reached out and touched Jesus' clothes she was instantly healed.[72]

Additionally, the father of a twelve-year-old girl came to Jesus saying, "My little daughter is at the point of death. Come lay your hands on her so that she will live." Jesus agreed to go with this man, but on their way someone ran up and said, "You're

---

69 John 3:19; Matthew 7:11, 26:63–64; Mark 14:61–62.
70 Mark 1:31.
71 Mark 2:11; Luke 5:24.
72 Mark 5:25–34.

too late. The little girl died." Jesus said, "Don't be afraid. Just believe." And when they arrived at the house, Jesus took her by the hand and sweetly said to her, "Little girl, I say to you, arise." And the girl got up and started walking.[73]

Jesus healed all kinds of sick people of their diseases.[74] He opened the ears of a deaf man so he could hear and opened the eyes of blind men so they could see.[75]

The people who saw these miracles were amazed. They said things like:

> *We've never seen anything like this.*[76]
> *He has done all things well.*[77]
> *Is not this the carpenter, the son of Mary?*[78]

The Gospel of John tells us that Jesus' miracles were signs, signs that pointed to who He was.[79] They were intended to authenticate His identity as the Son of God.[80] But in addition to His miracles, the best test of His truthfulness was how did Jesus respond when everything was on the line? In other words, how did He suffer and die?

---

73   Mark 5:21–43.
74   Mark 1:34.
75   Mark 7:32-35; Matthew 9:27-30
76   Matthew 9:33.
77   Mark 7:37.
78   Mark 6:3.
79   John 2:11, 23; 3:2; 4:48; 6:2, 26; 7:31; 9:16; 11:47; 20:30.
80   D. Martyn Lloyd-Jones, *Authority* (Carlisle, Pa.: Banner of Truth, 1984), 20.

They Know Not What They Do

The religious leaders hated Jesus. To them He was a religious nuisance who was stealing their thunder. He was "too dynamic to be safe," and they wanted Him extinguished.[81] So they secretly arrested Him, and while most of Jerusalem slept, Jesus Christ was on trial before the whole council of chief priests, elders, and scribes.[82] Many false accusations were made against Him, but when the witnesses couldn't agree, the high priest finally questioned Jesus himself.[83]

"I adjure you by the living God, tell us if you are the Christ, the Son of God?" Caiaphas demanded.[84]

"I am," Jesus said, "and you will see the Son of Man seated at the right hand of Power, and coming with the clouds of heaven."[85]

"He has uttered blasphemy," cried Caiaphas. "What is your judgment?"[86]

Outraged, the religious leaders angrily spit on Jesus, mocked Him, and punched Him. That dark night, they condemned Jesus to the death penalty.[87] A few hours later, at dawn, Jesus was brought to trial before the Roman governor over the province of Judea.

---

81 Dorothy Sayers, *Letters to a Diminished Church* (Nashville: W Publishing Group, 2004), 4.
82 Mark 14:35.
83 Mark 14:56.
84 Matthew 26:63.
85 Mark 14:62.
86 Matthew 26:65–66.
87 Mark 14:65.

"You will not speak to me?" Pilate said to Jesus. "Do you not know that I have authority to release you and authority to crucify you?"

Jesus answered him, "You would have no authority over me at all unless it had been given you from above."[88]

Pilate asked Him, "Do you not hear how many things they testify against you?"[89]

But Jesus made no further answer, so that Pilate was amazed.[90]

Jesus was facing crucifixion, and under the Roman Empire, people feared the cross. Historians from the time of Jesus tell us that crucifixion was "the most wretched of deaths."[91] In the ancient world, the cross was offensive, a sign of the greatest punishment and humiliation.[92] Crucifixion was often a means of "breaking the will of conquered peoples and of bringing mutinous troops under control."[93] Crucifixion was the death of slaves, thieves, prostitutes, and rebels. It was so gruesome that most ancient writers avoided describing it.[94] Yet in the face of the cross, Jesus did now waver; He did not recant; He did not apologize for His claims. Pilate questioned if he was making the right decision concerning Jesus' fate; however, the people prevailed by shouting, "Crucify Him, crucify Him!"[95]

---

88   John 19:10–11.
89   Matthew 27:13.
90   Mark 15:4–5.
91   Martin Hengel, *Crucifixion in the ancient world and the folly of the message of the cross* (Philadelphia : Fortress Press, 1977), 8.
92   Hengel, *Crucifixion*, 22.
93   Hengel, *Crucifixion*, 46.
94   Hengel, *Crucifixion*, 25, 38.
95   John 19:6–12.

Pilate handed Jesus to a battalion of around 600 soldiers for a preliminary beating—His second in the span of a few hours. Victims of crucifixion were first brutalized by what the Bible calls "flogging" or "scourging."[96] The Romans were experts in torture, and before a crucifixion they would flog their victims so that they would be too weak to kick or fight back when they were being nailed to the cross.[97] The soldiers stripped Jesus naked and tied His hands to an upright post. Then a short whip called a "flagrum" made of several leather cords, "in which small iron balls or sharp pieces of sheep bones were tied" was violently swung to smack against Jesus' bare back, butt, and legs.[98] The iron balls pounded into Jesus' flesh, severely bruising His body, while the pieces of bone ripped open the skin and tissues of His back.

The Journal of the American Medical Association published an article in 1986 describing the medical impact on Jesus' body, noting that "As the flogging continued, the lacerations would tear into the underlying skeletal muscles and produce quivering ribbons of bleeding flesh. Pain and blood loss generally set the stage for circulatory shock."[99] Next, the group of hostile soldiers twisted together a crown of thorns, pressed it into Jesus' scalp, and then struck Him in the head with a reed. They clothed Him in a purple robe, mocked Him, spit on Him, and

---

96   Mark 15:15; John 19:1.

97   Nabeel Qureshi Lecture "*Jesus of Islam vs. Jesus of Christianity*," (April 21, 2012), http://
     open.biola.edu/resources/jesus-of-islam-vs-jesus-of-christianity

98   William D. Edwards, Wesley J. Gabel, and Floyd E. Hosmer, "On the Physical Death of
     Jesus Christ," *Journal of the American Medical Association* 255, no. 11 (March 21, 1986).

99   Edwards, Wesley, and Hosmer, "On the Physical Death of Jesus Christ."

beat Him again.[100] At last they marched Him out to publicly crucify Him.

The soldiers placed a 75-pound crossbar on His shredded shoulders and demanded He march to The Place of the Skull.[101] By this time, Jesus was too weak to carry the cross, so another man, Simon the Cyrene, was forced to bear it. When they arrived at the spot, five-to- seven-inch nails, like railroad spikes, were pounded through Jesus' wrists and feet.[102] Again, a doctor describes this process, saying, "the driven nail would crush or sever the rather large sensorimotor median nerve. The stimulated nerve would produce excruciating bolts of fiery pain in both arms."[103] Now immobilized, Jesus was again stripped naked, and His cross was tilted upright for all to see.[104] His humiliation was complete.

While Jesus hung between heaven and earth, each breath was struggle. His body weight pulled against His outstretched arms, impeding His ability to exhale.[105] For three straight hours, the only way Jesus could breathe was to push up on the nail driven through His feet, thus allowing His lungs to collapse.[106] His mangled back continued to scrape against the splintery wood of the cross. Breathing hurt. Everything hurt. There was

---

100 Mark 15:18.
101 John 19:17; Edwards, Gabel, and Hosmer, "On the Physical Death of Jesus Christ."
102 Edwards, Gabel, and Hosmer, "On the Physical Death of Jesus Christ."
103 Edwards, Gabel, and Hosmer, "On the Physical Death of Jesus Christ."
104 John 19:23; Edwards, Gabel, and Hosmer, "On the Physical Death of Jesus Christ"; Sayers, *The Man Born To Be King*, 300; Charles H. Spurgeon, *C. H. Spurgeon The Early Years*, (Edinburgh: Banner of Truth Trust, 1962), 1:90; Qureshi, *Jesus of Islam vs. Jesus of Christianity*.
105 Edwards, Gabel, and Hosmer, "On the Physical Death of Jesus Christ."
106 Qureshi, *Jesus of Islam vs. Jesus of Christianity*.

no relief. The pain of crucifixion was so unequaled that a new word had to be invented to describe it—excruciating—which in Latin literally means, "out of the cross."[107]

At this point the crowds who once loved His preaching now walked by and insulted Jesus with hatred.

"Save yourself, and come down from the cross!" shouted the chief priests.[108]

"You're the Christ, O King of Israel? Come down now from the cross. We want to see and believe," added the scribes caustically.[109]

"He saved others, but He can't even save Himself."[110]

"Need a little wine, King?" said a soldier who pressed a nasty sponge dripping with sour wine against Jesus' lips.[111]

If Jesus was simply a pious man and no more, what we might expect in this moment would be for Him to cry out, "I'm innocent. This is injustice!"

But that's not what happened.

Instead, dripping with blood and gasping for air, Jesus prayed for His enemies. He knew His death was a sacrifice for sin, and Jesus prayed for grace to be shown to His murderers and mockers.[112] Jesus said aloud,

---

107   Edwards, Gabel, and Hosmer, "On the Physical Death of Jesus Christ."
108   Mark 15:30.
109   Mark 15:32.
110   Mark 15:31.
111   Luke 23:36.
112   Mark 10:45.

Father, forgive them, for they know not what they do.[113]

Who among us could do this? Neither you, nor I could have ever prayed such a prayer from the cross. Even the greatest religious teachers do not have this depth of compassion. Again we're bound to ask: Who is this man?

To make sure Jesus was dead, a professional executioner drove a spear up through Jesus' side, piercing His heart. Out spilled blood and water—Jesus was dead.[114]

This is no myth or metaphor. History's unanimous testimony is that Jesus died on the cross. Jewish, Gentile, and Christian historians all attest to the fact that Jesus really died by crucifixion.[115] Jesus really suffered the punishment of a hardened criminal, and He really died.[116] But that's not where His story ends.

We Have Seen the Lord

In the final year of Jesus' life, He repeatedly told His disciples He would suffer, die, and rise again.[117] He said to them:

See, we are going up to Jerusalem, and the Son of Man will be delivered over to the chief priests and the scribes, and they will condemn Him to death and deliver Him over to the Gentiles. And they will mock Him and spit

---

113   Luke 23:34.
114   John 19:33–35.
115   Qureshi, *Jesus of Islam vs. Jesus of Christianity.*
116   Hengel, *Crucifixion,* 83.
117   Mark 8:31–32; 9:9, 12, 31; 14:28.

on Him, and flog Him and kill Him. And after three
days He will rise.[118]

And three days after Jesus' death, a few women went to His tomb to say their final goodbyes, but what they found was that the stone had already been rolled away from the tomb's entrance. The tomb was empty, except for an angel who appeared to them and said:

Why do you seek the living among the dead? He is not
here, but has risen. Remember how He told you, while
He was still in Galilee, that the Son of Man must be
delivered into the hands of sinful men and be crucified
and on the third day rise.[119]

Shocked, the women ran back and told the disciples what they had seen. Their leader, Peter, ran to the tomb to verify the news. When Peter looked in, he saw an empty tomb with Jesus' burial cloths folded up and lying there.[120] Later that evening, while the disciples were gathered together, Jesus appeared to them, and He showed them His hands and His side.[121] He was alive, just as He said.

---

118   Mark 10:33–34.
119   Luke 24:5–7.
120   Luke 24:12; John 20:6–7.
121   John 20:19–20.

Over the next forty days Jesus appeared to His followers in groups as small as two and as big as 500.[122] They went around saying, "We have seen the Lord."[123] And they had.

The Good News!

These are the facts. But what do they mean *for us*? Well, we must begin with the bad news. The Bible says we are born dead in our sins.[124] This means you never have to teach a child to lie or be selfish or go their own way—that's just part of the original packaging. "Wherever we direct our view," William Wilberforce wrote, "we discover the melancholy proofs of our depravity; whether we look to ancient or modern times, to barbarous or civilized nations, to the conduct of the world around us, or the monitor within the breast; whether we read, or hear, or act, or think, or feel" we're broken beyond our own fixing.[125]

The doctrine of sin is the easiest doctrine to prove, but the hardest one to accept. But once we accept it, as Wilberforce said, and "have formed a true notion of [our] lost and help-less state, [we] will most gladly listen to the sound, and most justly estimate the value of such a deliverance."[126] So if you can come to the table an honest sinner, we can do business. If you're ready to acknowledge your depravity and admit you're

---

122   1 Corinthians 15:6.

123   John 20:25.

124   Psalm 51:5; Ephesians 2:1.

125   William Wilberforce, *A Practical View of Christianity*, (Peabody, Mass.: Hendrickson, 1996), 20.

126   Wilberforce, *Practical View*, 27.

not good enough to merit heaven, then please listen, I bring you good news of a great joy that will be for all the people![127]

The message of the Bible is this: BELIEVE IN JESUS! Eternal salvation is a free offer from a God who is rich in mercy and great in love.[128] Though sin has infected us with a disease we cannot cure, by Jesus' wounds we are healed.[129] Though our sin condemns us, Jesus died to set us free.[130] He was pierced for our transgressions and crushed for our iniquities.[131] Jesus became our substitute and died in our place for our sin.[132] The one who is sinless and perfect took our punishment upon Himself. In Jesus we're counted righteous before God.[133] We don't get what we deserve. There's been a great exchange.

"Believe in the Lord Jesus and you will be saved," says the Bible.[134] It doesn't say you *might* be saved or you *hope* to be saved or if-you-do-enough-good-deeds-to-outweigh-your-bad-ones then you'll be saved. It says BELIEVE IN JESUS and you *will* be saved. In another place, the Bible says, "If you confess with your mouth that Jesus is Lord and believe in your heart that God raised Him from the dead, you *will* be saved."[135] This means no matter how dirty you feel, Jesus' blood is able to cleanse you from all unrighteousness.[136] This means where our

---

127   Luke 2:10.
128   Ephesians 2:4.
129   Isaiah 53:5.
130   Romans 8:1.
131   Isaiah 53:5.
132   1 Corinthians 15:3.
133   2 Corinthians 5:21.
134   Acts 16:31.
135   Romans 10:9.
136   Hebrews 9:14; 1 John 1:9.

sins are multiplied, His grace abounds all the more.[137] Even our darkness is not dark to Him. The night is as bright as the day.[138] Listen, Jesus is famous for His grace.[139]

Even now Jesus appears in the presence of God on our behalf and pleads our case as, "Not guilty."[140] Though Satan stands to accuse us, reminding us of all our sins, the Lord Jesus rebukes him saying, "He belongs to me.[141] I took his punishment. On the cross I bore his shame, his filth, his guilt, his perversion, and all his sins.[142] I took the wrath that he deserves.[143] His record of debt has been canceled and nailed to the cross."[144] And God stamps your file: JUSTIFIED![145]

When Jesus said from the cross, "It is finished," our salvation was complete forever.[146] This means our salvation in Jesus is invincible, indestructible, unshakeable, eternal, and guaranteed.[147] No one can condemn us when He, who rose from death, intercedes for us.[148] None can stand against us, when Jesus stands for us.[149] Nothing can separate us from the love of Him who conquered the world.[150] Neither death, nor life, nor angels, nor rulers, not the present or the future, nor powers, nor

---

137 Romans 5:20.
138 Psalm 139:12.
139 John 1:14; 2 Corinthians 13:14; 2 Thessalonians 3:18.
140 Hebrews 9:24; 1 John 2:1.
141 Romans 1:6.
142 Isaiah 53:5; 2 Corinthians 5:21.
143 1 John 4:10.
144 Colossians 2:14.
145 Romans 5:9; 3:24.
146 John 19:30.
147 Hebrews 12:28; Ephesians 1:14.
148 Romans 8:34.
149 Romans 8:31–32.
150 John 16:33; Revelation 3:21.

height nor depth, nor anything else in all creation will be able to separate us from the love of God in Christ Jesus our Lord.[151] Jesus is able to save to the uttermost those who draw near to God through Him, and whoever comes to Him, He will never cast out.[152]

Jesus' salvation is all a gift of grace. The Bible says, "We all have sinned and fall short of the glory of God and are justified by His grace as a *gift*, through the redemption that is in Christ Jesus."[153] This is not our own doing, it is the *gift* of God.[154] What we deserve is death; for the wages of sin is death, but the free *gift* of God is eternal life in Christ Jesus our Lord.[155] As Wilberforce wonderfully said, Jesus is "our patron and benefactor and friend, 'who loved us and *gave* Himself for us.'"[156]

Let your heart by gripped by the one who died and gave Himself for you. This is who Jesus is— He's the Light of the World. He's the Lord of glory! He's the King of kings and Lord of lords. He's Immanuel, the Lamb of God, our High Priest, our Advocate with the Father, the Alpha and Omega, the Head of the Church, and the Savior of the World. Jesus is who He says He is, and we are invited to worship Him now and forever.[157]

And one day, when this life is over, those who love Him will see Him face to face. On that day Jesus will wipe away all tears, mourning, crying, and pain. And in the end, heaven and earth

---

151   Romans 8:35, 38–39.
152   Hebrews 7:25; John 6:3.7
153   Romans 3:23–24.
154   Ephesians 2:8.
155   Romans 6:23.
156   Wilberforce, *Practical View*, 40; Galatians 2:20.
157   1 Corinthians 2:8; Revelation 14:7.

will erupt in worship and quake with praise.[158] The crowd who worships Jesus on that day will be a diverse multitude that no one can number from every nation, tribe, people, and language. And Jesus' worshippers will sing and shout together:

> *"Salvation belongs to our God who sits on the throne,*
> *and to the Lamb! Worthy is the Lamb who was slain,*
> *to receive power and wealth and wisdom and might*
> *and honor and glory and blessing! To Him who sits on*
> *the throne and to the Lamb be blessing and honor and*
> *glory and might forever and ever!"*[159]

We need this truth of who Jesus is and what He's done to awaken our slumbering hearts and to dawn on our darkened world. The chaos and confusion in our world are because we see too little, not too much, of Jesus. The world needs the glory of Jesus Christ to been revealed. Monmouth, Lady Huntingdon, and Thornton knew this. They lived and died to know Jesus and make Him known. This is our mission too. This is the task of the church. This is the cause of the Christian. This is the gospel of Gospel Patronage.

---

158 1 Corinthians 13:12; Revelation 21:4, 22:4, 7:9.
159 Revelation 7:10; 5:12–13.

Write the vision;
Make it plain on tablets,
So he may run who reads it.

HABAKKUK 2:2

6 The Real Business of Life

A few months ago, I heard rumors of a woman who travels around the world proactively looking to support those who spread the gospel among the least-reached areas of the earth. "Who does that?" I said out loud. "I have to meet this woman." And a month later I did.

I learned that she was in her forties when she unexpectedly inherited a large portion of her family's business, worth millions of dollars. But unlike the winners of Publisher's Clearing House sweepstakes, her reaction was not joy; it was fear.

"Up until then I'd rarely given away five percent of my income. And even at that I thought I was giving away my life's savings. I was scared to death."

"Do you ever think of what you would have done with the money if you hadn't given it for gospel purposes?" I asked.

"It would have ruined me," she said without hesitation. "I know people who put their money in the bank and never touch it, never steward it. And lots of other people in my shoes spend it all and end up in debt. Others I know have lost their marriages over money problems, which includes having too much money. It would have ruined me. But now, after many years, the foundation I started gives away $300,000 each year, and I love it!"

It became clear to me that day that the calling of a Gospel Patron is a growth process, a journey of generosity. And wherever you are on that journey, I hope to help you take the next step. To do that, we'll crystalize the three components of a Gospel Patron.

1. Joyful Giving

Three years after that initial visit to Sydney, God opened a door for me to return. I wanted to ask Simon more about how Gospel Patronage gets lived out in our day.

One afternoon we sat in round wicker chairs on his deck, talking about the essence and practice of Gospel Patronage. We had both seen that from history to today, Gospel Patrons enjoy giving. For the Gospel Patron, giving is an opportunity, not an obligation; a blessing, not a burden. Even Jesus said, "It is more blessed to give than to receive."[1] It became clear that the first mark of a Gospel Patron is generous and joyful giving.

At this point, some of you might be thinking, "I'd be happy about giving too if I had more money." That sounds logical, but here we are confronted with the difference between the wisdom of this world and the wisdom of God. Worldly wisdom tells us to secure ourselves first, then give. But Jesus told a parable about a man who thought this way, saying,

> *The land of a rich man produced plentifully, and he*
> *thought to himself, "What shall I do, for I have nowhere*

---

1   Acts 20:35.

to store my crops?" And he said, "I will do this: I will tear down my barns and build larger ones, and there I will store all my grain and my goods. And I will say to my soul, Soul, you have ample goods laid up for many years; relax, eat, drink, be merry." But God said to him, "Fool! This night your soul is required of you, and the things you have prepared, whose will they be?" So is the one who lays up treasure for himself and is not rich toward God.[2]

Jesus cut right to the heart of the matter. To put ourselves first is foolish in God's eyes. Instead, Jesus tells us to put Him first. He praised a poor widow for this very thing.

Jesus looked up and saw the rich putting their gifts into the offering box, and he saw a poor widow put in two small copper coins. And he said, "Truly, I tell you, this poor widow has put in more than all of them. For they all contributed out of their abundance, but she out of her poverty put in all she had to live on."[3]

The widow's giving demonstrated that God was first in her life. Where her treasure was, there her heart was also.[4] The point here is that generous giving pleases God because it reveals that our hearts trust God and treasure Him. God is first.

---

2   Luke 12:16–21.
3   Luke 21:1–4.
4   Matthew 6:21.

Created for Good Works

But what does it mean to seek God's kingdom first? To put it simply, it means to live for eternity, to seek the things of heaven and not the things of earth. Colossians 3:1–2 helps us understand Jesus' words, explaining:

> *If then you have been raised with Christ, seek the things that are above, where Christ is, seated at the right hand of God. Set your minds on things that are above, not on things that are on earth.*

The word *seek* in this context means "to devote serious effort to realize one's desire or objective."[5] Athletes devote serious effort in order to win a race. Farmers devote serious effort in order to harvest a big crop. Soldiers devote serious effort in order to win a battle.[6] And Christians are called to devote serious effort in order to advance Jesus' kingdom.

Let me pause to ask: Is your life marked by serious effort to advance Jesus' kingdom? The reality is that most of us haven't been prepared for this kind of commitment, dedication, and discipline when it comes to our faith. William Wilberforce nailed this when he wrote, "No one expects to attain to the height of learning, or arts, or power, or wealth, or military glory, without vigorous resolution and strenuous diligence, and steady perse-

---

5   BDAG Greek-English Lexicon.

6   2 Timothy 2:4–6; Hebrews 12:1; 1 Corinthians 9:24–27.

verance. Yet we expect to be Christians without labor, study, or inquiry."[7]

The Bible is clear: we are not saved only to relax, retire, and wait for heaven. We are saved by grace, but saved to works. After God saves us He intends to use us in His work on earth. Notice this progression in Ephesians 2:8–10:

> *For by grace you have been saved through faith. And this is not your own doing; it is the gift of God, not a result of works, so that no one may boast. For we are His workmanship, created in Christ Jesus for good works, which God prepared beforehand, that we should walk in them.*

After we receive the gospel of grace, God wants you and me to go to work with Him. He adopts us and then invites us into the family business.

2. Gospel Proclamation

So what is God's family business? News, primarily. Christians are those who have been born again through Jesus' death and resurrection and then commissioned to carry the best news to as many people as possible from all nations, languages, and people groups of the earth. Jesus sends us out, saying:

---

7   Wilberforce, *Practical View*, 5–6.

> *You will be my witnesses …*
> *I am sending you …*
> *Go into all the world and proclaim the gospel …*
> *Repentance and forgiveness of sins should be proclaimed in [my] name to all nations …*
> *Go therefore and make disciples of all nations, baptizing them in the name of the Father, and of the Son, and of the Holy Spirit, teaching them to observe all that I have commanded you …*
> *And this gospel of the kingdom will be proclaimed throughout the whole world as a testimony to all nations, and then the end will come.*[8]

We have been given a glorious message of eternal importance to proclaim, and we read in the book of Acts that the first Christians were urgent in their efforts to proclaim it. Almost 120 times does Acts say the Christians were witnessing, proclaiming, speaking, teaching, preaching, explaining, testifying, persuading, proving, disputing, declaring, reasoning, admonishing, expounding, and trying to convince people about their risen Savior. Jesus first calls us to Himself, and then He calls us to exert serious effort to get His message out to the world.

Therefore, the second mark of a Gospel Patron is their strong commitment to spread the Word of God. There are many good things that need to be done in our world, many good causes that need support, but proclaiming the gospel is exclusive to

---

8   Acts 1:8; John 20:21; Mark 16:15; Luke 24:47; Matthew 28:18–20; Matthew 24:14.

the people of God. No one else will do it, and no one else will fund it.

For this reason, before a Gospel Patron partners with someone, the first question that should be asked is, "What do you believe?" In other words, "What message are you spreading? Is it the message of the Bible? Is it the gospel of Jesus Christ?"

Once a bishop complained to Lady Huntingdon's son Francis about all the chapels his mother was building, saying: "I wish you would speak to Lady Huntingdon. She has just erected a preaching place close to my palace wall."

"Gladly," said Francis, "but will you do me the favor to inform me what to urge, for my mother really believes the Bible."[9]

This deep commitment to the Bible fueled Lady Huntingdon to construct places for men to preach it. It fueled Monmouth to risk and suffer imprisonment on behalf of Tyndale's translation project. And it compelled Thornton to buy up the rights to church pulpits and appoint Bible-believing men to preach in those pulpits.

The pattern of history is that God raises up preachers and patrons to work together to spread His word. Some will speak and others will support, but both are partners in the gospel.

3. Personal Involvment

I asked Simon more about his patronage partnerships, and he shared with me how they require an investment not just of money, but also of time. We see this in the lives of Monmouth,

---

9   Cook, *Selina*, 344.

Lady Huntingdon, and Thornton too. Thomas Scott wrote that Thornton, "not only contributed his money, but he devoted his time and thoughts very much to the same object: doing good was the great business of his life and may more properly be said to have been his occupation than even his mercantile engagements."[10]

The third mark of a Gospel Patron is their deeply personal involvement in the work of the gospel. At its core, Gospel Patronage is about true partnerships. Gospel Patrons not only give money, they also give themselves. For Jesus' Gospel Patrons, Mary, Joanna, and Susanna, this meant joining Him on His preaching tours. For other patrons I know, this looks like carving out time to visit the missionaries they support.

"It's has been a life of joy and adventure," said one patron. "And one of the investments we've made in our kids is to travel and let them see what God is doing."[11]

For you, personal involvement could mean a monthly meeting with the church-planter you partner with to say, "Tell me about your work. How is it going? Where do you need help?" No doubt this kind of conversation happened when biblical patrons like Lydia and Gaius and Priscilla and Aquila came alongside the pastors and missionaries they hosted in their homes.[12]

In the ultimate example of Gospel Patronage, we see that God came among us, walked our dusty streets, ate our food, and

---

10 Thomas Scott, *The Love of Christ, the Source of Genuine Philanthropy* (J. Johnson, 1791).

11 Alan Barnhart, Biola University Leadership Lecture Series, "Starting at the Finish Line," (September 17, 2013), http://open.biola.edu/resources/becoming-kingdom-investors.

12 Lydia, Acts 16:14–15; Gaius, 3 John 5–8; Priscilla and Aquila, 1 Corinthians 16:19.

got personally involved in our lives. God invested Himself in the spread of the gospel. So should we.

The Real Business of Life

In 1963 a little book called *The Master Plan of Evangelism* surprised everyone when it went through more than sixty print runs and sold several million copies. In his conclusion, author Robert Coleman wrote, "The world is desperately seeking someone to follow. That they will follow someone is certain, but will that person know the way of Christ?"[13] The answer for much of our world is, "No, they don't know the way of Christ."

They can't follow Jesus because they've never heard the truth about Him. This is the case even in the countries most often considered "Christian nations." Jason Mandryk, in a book named *Operation World*, reports that "America's massive cultural and social influence makes it the world's greatest force for good and its greatest purveyor of sin. The American church needs revival."[14]

Of the United Kingdom, Mandryk writes, "The steep decline of organized Christianity in the UK is almost unparalleled in Europe. In England only 6% of people regularly attend church. The sense that all is not well pervades the country."[15]

Similar challenges are noted in Australia. "While over two-thirds of Australians identify themselves in some way as

---

13   Robert Coleman, *The Master Plan of Evangelism* (Grand Rapids, Mich.: Baker, 2005), 116.
14   Jason Mandryk, *Operation World: The Definitive Prayer Guide to Every Nation* (Colorado Springs: Biblica, 2010), 864.
15   Mandryk, *Operation World*, 852, 857.

Christian, only 10% regularly attend church. Almost all mainline churches face stagnation or decline, and growth even among evangelicals has slowed."[16]

When we zoom out to consider the rest of the world, researchers report the shocking truth that more than 7,000 people-groups have never heard of Jesus and have no one to tell them about Him.[17] Almost three billion people cannot call upon the God who saves because they have never heard of Him. Unless someone goes to them, they will continue to worship and serve created things rather than the Creator God.

The world is waiting. Our God is calling. And the testimony of history's great men is consistent.

King Solomon said, "He who wins souls is wise."[18]

The prophet Daniel said, "Those who turn many to righteousness [will shine] like the stars forever and ever."[19]

The Lord Jesus said, "For the Son of Man came to seek and save the lost."[20]

The apostle Paul said, "I have become all things to all people that by all means I might save some."[21]

George Whitefield said, "My one design is to bring poor souls to Jesus Christ."[22]

John Newton said, "To be useful to one soul is of more im-

---

16   Mandryk, *Operation World*, 119.
17   Joshua Project, www.joshuaproject.net.
18   Proverbs 11:30 (NIV).
19   Daniel 12:3.
20   Luke 19:10.
21   1 Corinthians 9:22.
22   Dallimore, *George Whitefield*, 1:561.

portance than the temporal prosperity of a whole nation."[23]

Charles Spurgeon said, "Our great object of glorifying God is to be mainly achieved by the winning of souls. We must see souls born unto God."[24]

C. S. Lewis said, "The glory of God, and, as our only means to glorifying Him, the salvation of human souls, is the real business of life."[25]

God uses people to save people. Will you join Him? Will you give your whole life to this? This is the real business of life!

The Next Step

I've marked out the lanes; now I hope you'll run. You don't need to be fast or have endurance. You don't have to run anybody else's race. Your job is to take the next step.

Monmouth began by going to church to hear an unusual preacher. Lady Huntingdon wrote a letter to a well-known evangelist inviting him to her house. John Thornton rode his horse sixty miles to listen to a former slave-trader teach the Bible. What about you? What is your next move?

Gospel Patrons have often gone unnoticed in the pages of Scripture and history, and perhaps that's how it should be. But maybe this book can resurrect their stories, if only for a little while, so that we might reclaim what they lived for. They car-

23   John Newton to Mrs. Lucy Thornton, January 21, 1777.
24   C. H. Spurgeon, *Lectures To My Students* (Grand Rapids: Mich.: Zondervan, 1954), 337.
25   C. S. Lewis, "Christianity and Culture" in *Christian Reflections* (Grand Rapids, Mich.: Eerdmans, 1967), 14.

ried the gospel forward in their generation. Will we continue to carry it in ours?

The good news is that we know Gospel Patronage is already happening. This book and my years of research and writing happened because a Gospel Patron shared these stories, because a Gospel Patron took a risk with me to tell these stories. And many more modern stories could, should, and will be told. But the next chapter is yours to write. Will the next generations be telling your story? Will eternity be telling your story?

God is not done writing history. He has prepared a part for you to play. It's your move.

Afterword

By Simon Pillar
Managing Director of Pacific Equity Partners

As we read these histories of Gospel Patrons of the past, we are both inspired and intimidated. They are wonderful stories of how God in His gracious providence brought together Tyndale and Monmouth, Whitefield and Lady Huntingdon and Newton and Thornton in deep and affecting relationships that changed the world forever. The question we may be asking though is how relevant are they to us?

We may feel *financially* inadequate. The patrons in this book were people of means. It can be hard to relate to the scale of their generosity and the level of their commitment to those they supported, but we need not be the richest merchant in England or a member of the aristocracy to be a Gospel Patron. Last year, John and I attended a church-planting conference in Australia where we heard the story of a young woman, I'll call Jenny. One evening at Jenny's church in Sydney a ministry leader announced that he and his family were planning to move to New Zealand to plant a church. That same evening Jenny announced to her parents that she was going to move with them. Jenny knew the demands of ministry and she wanted to support their family with the practicalities of moving and establishing their life in a new city so they could focus on gospel proclamation. Jenny's decision came with a substantial personal cost as she was a student at a top Sydney university and the move to Auckland meant she would not graduate. It was her heart for gospel ministry which drove her joyful and sacrificial giving in the context of a deep relational commitment to the church-planter and his family. This was Gospel Patronage, not predicated on the mobilization of wealth or networks but on a love for Jesus and a heart for the lost. Gospel Patronage is not just the domain of the wealthy.

We may feel *spiritually* inadequate to the task. The stories of Monmouth, Lady Huntingdon and Thornton evidence a seemingly inexhaustible passion to see the gospel proclaimed, but they were no plastic saints. They were people just like us, fallen, flawed and prone to failure. We know less of Monmouth than we do of the others, but for all of Lady Huntingdon's wisdom, vision and generosity she was also strong-willed to a fault and had a controlling personality. Thornton's relationship with his oldest son was tense and he had a reputation for irascibility. And yet how richly they were used by God!

These stories from history are important because they encourage us to look beyond the inadequacies we might feel in our own circumstances and take seriously the challenge to be Gospel Patrons. There is nothing more strategic than planning for eternity. Gospel Patronage is strategic because at its heart is gospel proclamation and it is therefore an investment in eternity that will bear eternal rewards. Importantly though, in addition to being strategic, Gospel Patronage is also good for our own souls. We shall find that by committing ourselves relationally to a ministry whose focus is the Word of God we shall have the opportunity to share in the joys, as well as the trials, of those with whom we are in partnership. As Gospel Patrons, we too learn joyful dependence on the Lord Jesus and with it cheerful and open-handed generosity.

The risk of any topical book which hopes to challenge its readers to action is that it becomes too prescriptive. John has avoided this, rather helping us to see the three marks of Gospel Patronage that delineate it from conventional philanthropy. The essence of Gospel Patronage is joyful, generous and sacrificial giving; a priority on Word ministry; and a deep relational commitment. The last of these implies that it is about more than just money. It involves time, talents, networks and wrestling in prayer. It is up to each of us to work out how we apply these broad principles in our own circumstances. We may be in a position to partner with an individual church-planter or to seed a whole new church-planting network. We may be called to stand with the young pastor in our own city who is painstakingly and slowly discipling men on the fringes of society or to establish a new long-term mission work in Africa or South America. The scale of our patronage is less important that its scope, but perhaps most important is that we take the next step. The examples in this book are extraordinary in their ripple effects down through the centuries to us today. And yet each relationship began with one small step. Undoubtedly, Monmouth,

Lady Huntingdon and Thornton each saw something in the men they backed which convinced them to take that first step. If our desire is to see millions come into a saving relationship with God through Jesus, who are the men and women we are going to back and how can we help them shape their ministries for maximum impact?

In Chapter 1 John recalls our meeting in Sydney in 2009. The ripple effect of that meeting is this book. Along the way a deep and cherished friendship has formed. Only God knows where the story goes from here. But if the re-telling of these stories leads you to develop just one Gospel Patronage partnership, there is no telling how great may be the ripple effect in centuries to come, and the world truly may never be the same again...

Acknowledgements

I dedicated this book to Jesus, who is the ultimate Gospel Patron. But He has also graciously brought me many others along the way. Thank you to my wife, Renée, who believed in me and this project from the very beginning. I am a better man and this is a better book because of you. It never would have happened without your strong and faithful friendship.

Thank you to Simon Pillar for sharing this vision with me for the first time. You've become a great friend along the way, a man I deeply admire, and only heaven will reveal the global impact of your Gospel Patronage.

Thank you to my Gospel Patron who will remain anonymous. You have out-given them all and truly are the Gospel Patron of Gospel Patronage. May this project bear fruit we can rejoice over for many years to come.

Thank you to Dan Peck. I have not found the end to your generosity and don't imagine I ever will. Your enthusiasm for these stories has been exactly the boost my faith needed so many times. Thank you to my parents for supporting all my dreams. From a young age you both gave me the green light to dream big and I don't plan on stopping any time soon.

Thank you to John-Mark Warkentin and Adam Shaeffer. I've loved the partnership and hope this is just the beginning. Thank you to all my Think-tank guys. May God make us like the Clapham Circle, servants of the suffering and proclaimers of the only message that can save.

Thank you to the many people who contributed to the research, read advanced copies, wrote endorsements, prayed for me, and jumped in to back the Kickstarter project so we could produce a premium quality book that we hope will help the message of Gospel Patrons speak of His awesome deeds from one generation to the next.

Lastly, to my kids, Willow and Malachi. It will be a few years before you can read this, but your Ababa loves you and is praying that you'll find your part to play in carrying the gospel forward in your generation.

About the Author

JOHN RINEHART studied business at Biola University and later got his MDiv from Talbot School of Theology. In 2010 he became an elder at Grace Evangelical Free Church in La Mirada, California and in 2011 started a mercy-ministry there called Grace Foodbank that now serves thousands of people each year.

Most recently, he and his wife, Renée, adopted a boy and a girl from Ethiopia and are also planting a church in Fullerton, California, where he preaches regularly.

To research *Gospel Patrons*, John traveled to England and Australia, transcribed 200-year-old letters from the libraries at Cambridge and Oxford, and interviewed scholars, historians, and modern-day patrons. *Gospel Patrons* is his first book.

For more information, or to contact John Rinehart,
visit www.gospelpatronage.com

gos • pel pa • trons, *noun.* **1.** people who resource and come alongside others to help them proclaim the gospel.